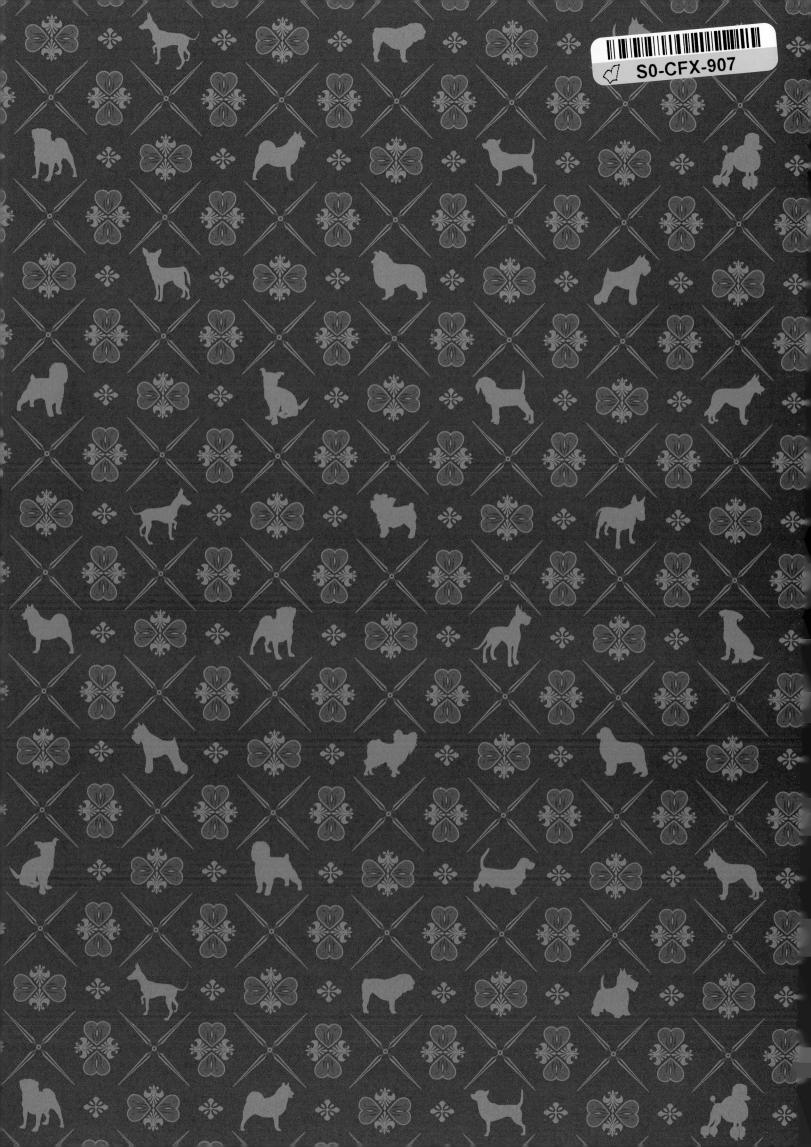

WINE DOGS
=Australia=

"If a dog's prayers were answered,
bones would rain from the sky."

PROVERB

ARCHIMEDES AND PHOEBE FIVE-YEAR-OLD HUNGARIAN VIZSLA AND SIX-YEAR-OLD RHODESIAN RIDGEBACK, MOORILLA, BERRIDALE, TAS

CONTENTS

SEPPELTSFIELD
~ EST 1851 ~

*NAUGHTIEST DEED: CHEWING THE
CORNERS OFF A SHEEPSKIN RUG
FAVOURITE TOY: LITTLE BLUE MONKEY
OWNERS: WARREN AND NICKY RANDALL
PET HATE: THE EXHAUST NOTE OF THE FERRARI
FAVOURITE FOODS: SALMON SASHIMI AND PISTACHIOS
OBSESSION: HUNTING RATS AROUND THE CHICKEN COOP*

*NAUGHTIEST DEED:
HUNTING NATIVE FEASTS
PET HATE: ANGRY PEOPLE
FAVOURITE FOODS: ROAST CHICKEN
AND MEDIUM-RARE FILLET STEAK
OWNERS: WARREN AND NICKY RANDALL
OBSESSIONS: POINTING AND CHASING RABBITS AT SEPPELTSFIELD
FAVOURITE PASTIME: BEING PHOTOGRAPHED WITH CELLAR DOOR CUSTOMERS*

FOREWORD

by Nick Stock

AS A BUSY WINE WRITER you visit a lot of wineries, which is a part of the job I really love. My first real memory of wine is when I was just seven years old. I was so fascinated by the big gear inside this one amazing winery my grandparents took me to in the Barossa Valley that I used to harass them to take me again and again. That winery turned out to be Seppeltsfield and all that gear is still there today.

These were my dog-loving grandparents (they had a Dachshund and a Cocker Spaniel) that didn't drink (my other grandparents made up for that) and yet they happily took me there time after time. That's actually where my whole fascination for wine was first born. They were awesome grandparents, I wonder if they ever thought I'd end up spending my working life in and around wine and wineries? I'm pretty sure they knew I'd get a dog.

When I visit wineries today I'm looking with very different eyes. I'm pretty much casing the joint, looking to see what's happening at every turn and I've developed a bit of a checklist. The way the vineyard looks is really important, it actually tells you a lot about the wines without even tasting them, so I always get out among the vines.

The way the winery looks is also really important but what I'm looking for there is very different to the vineyard. I'm trying to suss the vibe and the mood of the place and there's a bit of that workdesk psych test thing too, but more on a grand scale.

You can tell a lot about a winery by the level of tidiness (a real worry if it's too anal, but you also don't want a dog's breakfast), the memorabilia (again, not too much, it's a winery not a museum after all), the little reminders, things for inspiration, for a laugh and, of course, the playlist. I also case the winemaking gear out too, old habits; you know.

But the very first place I check out at any winery is actually the cellar door. It's a voyeuristic thing where I like to just rock in and see what everyone's up to, listen to what they're saying and check out what they're buying. I listen to the way the winery guys and girls talk about the wines they're serving, I look at the reactions and I also look for the dog!

Of course that's if the dog hasn't found me first. The unmeasured love of a dog when it makes a new friend, the wag of the tail, the offer to play fetch, to allow you to pat the back or, if you're really lucky, the belly – wine aside, these are the best things you can hope to encounter at a winery.

I have many fond memories of winery pooches. Years ago when visiting Pikes up in Clare the family set up on a blanket under a shady tree only to have the winery Labrador come galloping for a big rolling, Riesling-soaked landing. We still laugh about it.

Very recently I was out at Oakridge in the Yarra for a tasting and lunch with winemaker Dave Bicknell when his old and trusty Staffy, Larry (whose stocky, silvery appearance is uncannily similar to Dave himself), came swaggering in to join us like he was busting out some kind of four-legged John Wayne impersonation. Also just like Dave, old Larry doesn't get phased by much, he just does his thing in his own way and his own time.

I've actually come to worry about a winery that has no dog, it just doesn't seem right. Just like the vineyard and the cellar, a healthy and happy winery dog is a sign of a healthy and happy winery. I've also come to recognise that a great dog usually belongs to great people and where the people are great, the wine is rarely far behind.

Enjoy this latest edition of *Wine Dogs* and see you at cellar door!

NICK STOCK IS ONE OF AUSTRALIA'S MOST PROLIFIC WINE COMMENTATORS WHOSE INVOLVEMENT IN WINE STRETCHES WELL BEYOND WRITING TO RADIO AND TELEVISION BROADCASTING, WINE SHOW JUDGING, PUBLIC SPEAKING, EDUCATING AND WINEMAKING. HIS DOGGED PURSUIT OF GREAT WINE TAKES HIM ALL OVER THE PLACE AND HE'S COME TO RECOGNISE THAT WHEREVER GREAT WINE IS MADE, THERE'S USUALLY A GREAT DOG NEARBY. WWW.WINELENS.COM.AU

PET HATE: CAR WINDOWS
OBSESSION: CHASING BIRDS
OWNER: AMY SUTHERLAND SMITH
FAVOURITE TOY: A SQUEAKING TURDUCKEN
FAVOURITE PASTIMES: PLAYING FETCH AND DIGGING
FAVOURITE FOOD: HIS FOUR-YEAR-OLD (HUMAN) SISTER'S DINNER
NAUGHTIEST DEED: JUMPING OUT THE WINDOW OF A SPEEDING CAR

PET HATE: BEING LEFT AT HOME
FAVOURITE TOYS: SQUEAKY STUFFED TOYS
THAT NO LONGER HAVE FACES OR EARS
OBSESSION: RATTLING CAR KEYS WHICH
MEAN A CAR RIDE TO THE VINEYARD
OWNERS: STEPHEN AND PRUE HENSCHKE
FAVOURITE PASTIME: BEING PRUE'S SHADOW
NAUGHTIEST DEED: SNEAKING UNDER THE BIRD
NETTING TO EAT PRECIOUS 'HILL OF GRACE' GRAPES

LOTTE

TOBY

OWNERS: QUINN AND MARIE LIVINGSTONE
FAVOURITE PASTIMES: WAITING UNDER THE BBQ
AND SLEEPING (MINIMUM 14 HOURS A DAY)
FAVOURITE TOY: STUFFED GIRAFFE, NOW SADLY HEADLESS
FAVOURITE FOOD: ANYTHING FROM OFF THE BBQ AT FUNCTIONS
NAUGHTIEST DEEDS: BEGGING AT THE LOCAL PUB, SCHOOL AND CAFE
AND RUNNING OFF WITH THE WINE DOG PHOTOGRAPHER'S TREATS

PET HATE: LOUD NOISES
FAVOURITE TOY: RABBIT
FAVOURITE FOOD: RABBIT
OWNERS: JEN AND DAVID WRIGHT
FAVOURITE PASTIMES: CHASING RABBITS AND
PLAYING WITH ANGUS FROM SHOTTESBROOKE

NELLY

LOUIS

OWNERS: LUCY AND DARREN GOLDING
FAVOURITE PASTIMES: HANGING OUT
AT CELLAR DOOR AND CHASING BALLS
NAUGHTIEST DEED: IT INVOLVED ONE CHICKEN,
ONE PUPPY AND A WHOLE LOT OF FEATHERS
FAVOURITE TOY: ANYTHING THAT LOOKS LIKE A STICK
OBSESSION: PLAYING WITH STICKS THREE TIMES HIS SIZE
FAVOURITE FOODS: BONES AND THE OCCASIONAL PIECE OF CHEESE

OWNER: JOHN RYMILL
OBSESSION: JOHN RYMILL
FAVOURITE FOODS: CUPCAKES (SHARED WITH SMALL CHILDREN) OR DECEASED GOLDFISH FOUND FLOATING IN THE PONDS OUT THE FRONT OF CELLAR DOOR
FAVOURITE PASTIME: STARING LONGINGLY AT CUSTOMERS IN CELLAR DOOR FROM OUTSIDE
PET HATES: LIGHTNING, THUNDER AND BEING TOLD WHAT TO DO BY PEOPLE OTHER THAN JOHN

REG

PINOT

OBSESSION: STEALING CLEAN LAUNDRY
FAVOURITE TOY: LITTLE PINK PIG SOFT TOY
OWNERS: ANTON AND ABBY STADNICZENKO
NAUGHTIEST DEED: CHASING MAISIE THE CAT
PET HATE: ANTON AND ABBY GOING TO WORK
FAVOURITE FOODS: PIG EARS AND CHICKEN NECKS
FAVOURITE PASTIMES: BATHING AND GETTING LAZY ON THE COUCH

PET HATE: DISCIPLINE
OWNER: JEREMY FERGUSSON
FAVOURITE TOY: A 40CM-LONG PVC PIPE
FAVOURITE PASTIME: GREETING THE TOUR BUSES
NAUGHTIEST DEED: KEEPING THE RABBITS ON THEIR TOES
OBSESSIONS: VINTAGE WINE CLIPPINGS AND FOAM BOXES
FAVOURITE FOODS: CHICKEN NECKS AND MARROW BONE SCHMACKOS

SAPPHIRE

HAMISH

OWNER: JANE CAMPBELL
OBSESSION: TRYING TO GET
INTO THE LAND ROVER WHEN
JANE LEAVES FOR THE WINERY
FAVOURITE TOY: LIZZIE THE BLUE HEELER PUP
FAVOURITE FOODS: MARROW BONES AND BACON
NAUGHTIEST DEED: CHEWING OUTDOOR FURNITURE
PET HATE: HAVING HIS PAWS CHECKED FOR GRASS SEEDS

FAVOURITE TOY: TEDDY
FAVOURITE FOOD: FRESH MINCE
NAUGHTIEST DEED: CHASING THE CATS
OBSESSION: CHEWING HIS LEAD IN HALF
OWNERS: ANDREW AND ANEEKA HANIGAN
FAVOURITE PASTIME: CHASING ANYTHING THAT MOVES

ALBY

GRACIE

PET HATE: THE BRUSHCUTTER
OWNERS: VIV AND PHIL SNOWDEN
FAVOURITE TOY: LARGE BLUE KONG
NAUGHTIEST DEED: CHASING THE GEESE
FAVOURITE FOOD: ANYTHING CALLED A TREAT
OBSESSION: NIPPING AT HER OWNERS' HEELS
FAVOURITE PASTIME: GOING FOR WALKS TO CHECK THE VINEYARD

OWNER: SCOTT COMYNS
NAUGHTIEST DEED: FARTING
THEN LEAVING THE ROOM
OBSESSION: CHASING THE FOOTY
FAVOURITE TOY: SHERRIN FOOTBALL
PET HATES: LETTUCE, BEANS AND BROCCOLI
FAVOURITE PASTIME: SUNBAKING SPREADEAGLED
IN THE MIDDLE OF THE ROAD TO THE WINERY

DEXTER

SCOUT

OWNER: SAMANTHA CONNEW
FAVOURITE FOOD: MARROWBONE
FAVOURITE TOY: THE STUFFED KANGAROO THAT
WAS GIVEN TO SAM WHEN SHE GOT HER CITIZENSHIP
NAUGHTIEST DEED: RUNNING AROUND THE
HOUSE WITH THE END OF THE TOILET PAPER ROLL
OBSESSION: THE EARS OF MURPHY BROWN, THE LABRADOR
FAVOURITE PASTIME: CHASING CHICKENS AROUND THE YARD

OWNER: DANICA BETTENAY
FAVOURITE TOY: TUG-OF-WAR
FAVOURITE FOOD: REEF AND BEEF
NAUGHTIEST DEED: EATING EVERYTHING
PET HATE: BEING SMOTHERED WITH CUDDLES
FAVOURITE PASTIME: SLEEPING IN THE OLD SEA MINE
OBSESSIONS: OTHER DOGS AND SWIMMING IN THE LAKE

SONNY

AMERICAN LONG-LEGGED BEAGLE, 2 | **BETTENAY WINES** COWARAMUP, WA

SCOOBY

OWNER: CAROLYN STEVENS
PET HATE: THE WINE AGITATOR
FAVOURITE TOY: SQUEAKY GUMBOOT TOY
KNOWN ACCOMPLICE: HENRY THE DONKEY
FAVOURITE PASTIME: SLEEPING IN CAROLYN'S CHAIR
AFTER RUNNING THROUGH A MUDDY VINEYARD
OBSESSION: TOUCHING NOSES WITH HENRY THE DONKEY
NAUGHTIEST DEED: STEALING SOCKS FROM UNATTENDED GUMBOOTS

FAVOURITE TOY: BLUE CROCHETED BLANKET
OBSESSIONS: BABY MAX AND BELLY TICKLES
OWNERS: GREG COOLEY AND KELLI SHANAHAN
FAVOURITE FOOD: ANYTHING ANYONE ELSE HAS
KNOWN ACCOMPLICES: JACK, RUBY AND PHOEBE
NAUGHTIEST DEED: SHREDDING A LOUNGE CHAIR
PET HATE: BEING SEPARATED FROM GREG AND MAX
FAVOURITE PASTIME: GREETING/SNOUTING CUSTOMERS

MICKEY

EADIE

OWNERS: THE SEXTON FAMILY
FAVOURITE FOOD: KANGAROO POO
FAVOURITE PASTIME: RUNNING WITH PHIL
NAUGHTIEST DEED: BAILING UP KANGAROOS
OBSESSION: KEEPING THE CHICKENS COMPANY
PET HATE: BEING TIED UP DURING A FULL MOON
KNOWN ACCOMPLICE: PIRATE, THE SHETLAND PONY

OWNERS: DEB AND MAL REDMAN
NAUGHTIEST DEED: AIR HUMPING ONE
YEAR-OLD CHILDREN AT CELLAR DOOR
FAVOURITE PASTIME: SLEEPING (BUT WILL DRAG
HIMSELF OUT OF BED TO GREET THE VISITORS)
FAVOURITE FOOD: SCOTCH FILLET, MEDIUM RARE
PET HATES: WATER, SWIMMING AND LOUD NOISES
FAVOURITE TOYS: RUBBER RING AND ANYTHING WITH A BELL IN IT

TREVOR

RUDY

OWNER: VANESSA NEAL
FAVOURITE TOY: SOCKS
PET HATE: NOT BEING FED
OBSESSIONS: FOOD AND SOCKS
FAVOURITE PASTIME: PARADING AROUND
THE HOUSE WITH SOCKS IN HER MOUTH
NAUGHTIEST DEED: PUGWASHING (PREWASHING
THE DISHES IN THE DISHWASHER)

SHELBY

PET HATE: BATHTIME
OWNER: VANESSA NEAL
FAVOURITE TOY: HER DOGGY BED
FAVOURITE FOOD: GOURMET HUMAN FOOD
NAUGHTIEST DEED: BEING HOUDINI INCARNATE
AND ESCAPING AT ANY OPPORTUNITY
OBSESSION: LYING IN THE SUN WORKING ON HER TAN
FAVOURITE PASTIME: CUDDLES WITH NEW BABY MADISON

OWNERS: TOM KEELAN AND REBECCA WILLSON
FAVOURITE TOY: OLD ADAM WINE BARREL BUNGS
PET HATE: HER ARCH NEMESIS – BREMERTON THE CAT
NAUGHTIEST DEED: SNEAKING INTO CELLAR DOOR FOR A PAT
FAVOURITE PASTIME: PLAYING CATCH WITH KIDS ON THE WINERY LAWN

CHARLIE

"There is no psychiatrist in the world
like a puppy licking your face."

BERNARD WILLIAMS

OWNER: TIM FOLLETT
FAVOURITE TOY: SQUEAKY PIG
FAVOURITE FOOD: METTWURST
OBSESSION: TUMMY SCRATCHES
NAUGHTIEST DEED: DIGGING HOLES
KNOWN ACCOMPLICE: SISTER CHARLIE
FAVOURITE PASTIMES: EATING AND CHEWING SHOES

JESS

OWNER: PATRICK COWARD
OBSESSION: MUDDY DAMS
KNOWN ACCOMPLICES: SINDU,
JOLIE, DIVA, DOUGALL AND LILI
PET HATE: OWNER WITH A HANGOVER
FAVOURITE PASTIME: WELCOMING GUESTS
FAVOURITE TOY: ANYTHING THAT SQUEAKS
FAVOURITE FOOD: PORRIDGE WITH LOCAL HONEY
NAUGHTIEST DEED: DESTROYING A THREE-SEATER LOUNGE

PET HATE: VISITING THE VET
FAVOURITE FOOD: ANYTHING IN
HARRY'S BOWL, FOLLOWED BY HERS
OBSESSION: DUMPING DEAD ANIMAL
REMAINS ON THE FRONT DOORSTEP
OWNERS: STEPHEN AND LEANNE WEBBER
NAUGHTIEST DEED: CONSTANTLY DUMPING
DEAD ANIMAL REMAINS ON THE FRONT DOORSTEP

MISSY

PET HATE: THE CAT
OWNERS: STEPHEN AND LEANNE WEBBER
FAVOURITE PASTIMES: SLEEPING AND EATING
FAVOURITE FOODS: LEFTOVER STEAK AND PIZZA
NAUGHTIEST DEED: EATING A DUCK FROM OFF THE BBQ
OBSESSION: OFFERING PEOPLE LEAVES IN EXCHANGE FOR FOOD

HARRY

AUGIE

PET HATE: THE LAWNMOWER
FAVOURITE TOY: THE NOISIEST KIND
FAVOURITE PASTIME: ROUNDING UP THE CHOOKS
OWNERS: JARED STRINGER AND ALEXANDRA CAMATTA
OBSESSION: TEARING APART ANYTHING WITH STUFFING
KNOWN ACCOMPLICE: HIS BEST MATE, WINSTON THE CAVADOR
NAUGHTIEST DEED: STEALING SOCKS AND JOCKS BECAUSE HE KNOWS HE WILL BE CHASED

FERGIE

OWNER: MATT HARROP
FAVOURITE TOY: KIDS' SHOES
OBSESSION: HUNTING RABBITS
PET HATE: BEING TOLD WHAT TO DO
FAVOURITE FOODS: RABBIT AND CHICKEN
NAUGHTIEST DEED: CHASING TWO LAMBS INTO THE DAM
FAVOURITE PASTIME: CHASING ANYTHING SMALL AND FAST

FAVOURITE FOOD: WORK BOOTS
FAVOURITE TOY: DOUGLAS THE CAT
PET HATE: UNWILLING PLAYMATES
OBSESSION: WATER FROM THE HOSE
NAUGHTIEST DEED: A WORK IN PROGRESS
FAVOURITE PASTIME: CHASING BUTTERFLIES
AND OTHER WINGED CREATURES
OWNERS: SALLY BROWN AND ROWLY MILHINCH

SASHA

HUNTER

OWNER: TOM O'DONNELL
FAVOURITE TOY: TOILET ROLLS
FAVOURITE FOOD: PAPPADUMS
OBSESSION: PARADING STOLEN ITEMS
PET HATE: BEING DISTURBED WHILE SLEEPING
FAVOURITE PASTIME: CRUISING ON THE FORKLIFT
NAUGHTIEST DEED: RIPPING UP THE CARPET AND WAITING
FOR IT TO BE REPLACED BEFORE DOING IT AGAIN (3 TIMES)

OWNER: JUSTIN McNAMEE
FAVOURITE PASTIME: SLEEPING
IN THE FRONT SEAT OF THE PRADO
PET HATE: GARRY THE DOG WASHER
OBSESSION: ANYTHING REMOTELY EDIBLE
FAVOURITE TOY: ANY ITEM OF JUSTIN'S CLOTHING
NAUGHTIEST DEED: FARTING UNDER KERRIE'S DESK

PASCOE

BONNIE

OBSESSION: *LITTLE CHILDREN*
OWNERS: *THE REDHEAD FAMILY*
PET HATE: *BEING AWAY FROM THE ESTATE*
FAVOURITE TOYS: *CATS, BALLS AND VINE PRUNINGS*
NAUGHTIEST DEED: *HAVING HER PUPPIES IN A DEEP
DEN, WHERE THEY STAYED FOR TWO WHOLE WEEKS*
FAVOURITE PASTIME: *SHADOWING CREWS IN THE VINEYARD*

BELLE

OBSESSION: *SLEEPING*
OWNERS: *THE REDHEAD FAMILY*
FAVOURITE TOY: *A FRESH CARCASS*
PET HATES: *THUNDER AND GUNSHOTS*
NAUGHTIEST DEED: *STALKING CHICKENS*
FAVOURITE PASTIME: *SWIMMING IN THE DAM*

FAVOURITE TOY: A GIANT PINK FLEA
OWNERS: BRETT AND KERRY HOUSE
KNOWN ACCOMPLICE: ELVIS THE PUG
OBSESSIONS: BAXTER THE CAT AND FOOD
PET HATE: BEING LEFT AT HOME DURING VINTAGE
NAUGHTIEST DEED: NIPPING PEOPLE'S FEET TO GET ATTENTION

KACEE

TILLY

OWNER: SIMON KILLEEN
PET HATE: SQUEAKY TOYS
FAVOURITE FOOD: CHICKEN NECKS
OBSESSIONS: HUNTING AND CHASING RABBITS
NAUGHTIEST DEED: EATING A TRAY OF RAT BAIT
FAVOURITE PASTIME: GOING FOR RUNS WITH SIMON
KNOWN ACCOMPLICE: JULIETTE, THE FAT BORDER
COLLIE (IT'S A FAT AND SKINNY KIND OF RELATIONSHIP)

OWNER: WENDY KILLEEN
OBSESSION: PULLING HER
WOOLLEN BEDDING ONTO THE
LAWN AND TEARING IT TO SHREDS
FAVOURITE TOY: ZARA THE RUSSIAN BLUE KITTY
KNOWN ACCOMPLICES: MOLLY, TILLY AND ZARA
FAVOURITE PASTIME: DIGGING UP MOUSE HOLES
NAUGHTIEST DEED: EATING THE PET SILKY BANTAM
PET HATE: NOT BEING ALLOWED INSIDE AT NIGHT FOR A SMOOCH

JULIETTE

COOPER

OWNER: JOSH PFEIFFER
KNOWN ACCOMPLICE: BJ THE BORDER COLLIE
PET HATES: VACUUM CLEANERS AND BLOWER VACS
FAVOURITE TOYS: BIG STICKS, SOCCER BALLS AND BIGGER STICKS
OBSESSIONS: WILLIE WAGTAILS, MOTORBIKES, STICKS AND SOCCER BALLS
NAUGHTIEST DEED: STEALING SCOTCH FILLET STEAK FROM THE KITCHEN BENCH
FAVOURITE FOODS: CHEESE AND METTWURST, STOLEN FROM CUSTOMERS' PLATTERS

OWNER: SALLY PFEIFFER
PET HATE: AN EMPTY PELLET TROUGH
NAUGHTIEST DEED: POOPING IN THE PELLET TROUGH
FAVOURITE TOY: NORTH MELBOURNE (ROOS) FOOTBALL
FAVOURITE FOODS: ALMONDS AND WHISTLER MERLOT GRAPES
FAVOURITE PASTIME: PLAYING CHASEY WITH BUTTONS (HIS ROO MATE)

BANJO

OWNER: ROB QUENBY
PET HATE: BEING LEFT BEHIND
FAVOURITE FOOD: CAT BISCUITS
OBSESSION: WATCHING TEST CRICKET ON THE COUCH WITH ROB
FAVOURITE PASTIME: CHASING AND BARKING AT KANGAROOS IN HIS SLEEP
NAUGHTIEST DEED: EATING TWO TRAYS OF MUFFINS OFF THE BREAKFAST COUNTER

BUZZ

WEST CAPE HOWE

OWNER: GAVIN BERRY
FAVOURITE PASTIME: BARKING
WHILE GAV IS ON THE PHONE
NAUGHTIEST DEED: ACTING AS QUALITY
CONTROL, ESPECIALLY WITH HOMEMADE
SAUSAGES AND FRESH BREAD DOUGH
OBSESSION: GETTING HER BUTT SCRATCHED
FAVOURITE TOY: ANYTHING DEAD TO ROLL IN

BESSIE

XENA

OWNER: ROB ELLIS
OBSESSIONS: SLEEPING AND RABBITING
FAVOURITE PASTIME: MOTHERING PEPPER
FAVOURITE TOY: A TOY POSSUM, STOLEN FROM THE CUPBOARD
FAVOURITE FOOD: ANYTHING THAT COMES OFF SOMEONE'S PLATE
NAUGHTIEST DEED: TEACHING THE PUPPY TO STEAL EGGS FOR HER

OWNER: RUTH ELLIS
PET HATE: BEING LEFT ALONE
FAVOURITE PASTIME: RUNNING
FAVOURITE TOY: DAD'S CLOTHES
OBSESSIONS: RUNNING THEN
SLEEPING, RUNNING THEN SLEEPING
NAUGHTIEST DEED: STEALING EGGS FOR OTHER DOGS

PEPPER

KRUMPLI

FAVOURITE TOY: SOCCER BALL
FAVOURITE FOOD: PIZZA CRUSTS
OWNERS: MIKE BENNIE AND ALEX BIERI
OBSESSION: VISITING THE LOCAL BREWERY
NAUGHTIEST DEED: JUMPING INTO SYDNEY HARBOUR
THEN TRESPASSING THROUGH A HARBOUR-FRONT
MILLION-DOLLAR MANSION (VIA THE SWIMMING POOL)
FAVOURITE PASTIME: SWIMMING, SWIMMING, SWIMMING

the DOG with TERROIR

by Mike Bennie

I REALLY LIKED a winemaker-mate's dog, Ralfy. Ruffled, perm-like woolly coat set to neat curls. Happy, quiet demeanour. Loyalty of a serf. Tangled underfoot, then graceful in avoiding a boot. Dogged in chase of ball. Those intelligent, golden eyes.

He told me Ralfy was a 'small Curly Coated Retriever, I think', as he tapped on his can of beer and whacked another tennis ball deep into his vineyard. Ralfy methodically pursued, stalking each row of vine, weaving under the trellis.

I dutifully tapped those four words into a search engine and scoured the bowels of the Internet. Investigation led me to an online, enthusiasts' group for something called a Murray River Curly Coated Retriever. The user group chittered and chatted about their beloved, historical working dog breed with a fervour nigh on religious.

"Australia's oldest working dog breed." "The Americans who taught us how to use paddle steamers on the Murray River bred them up for duck hunting." "They bear a striking resemblance to the American Water Spaniel... but different." "A true heritage breed."

Krumpli tumbled out from an aeroplane, animal-courier box onto our feet as a ten-week-old puppy. She was the one wearing the red collar, the one that liked to nibble toes.

If I had a dollar for every time I've been stopped on the street and asked "What breed is that?" or "Is that a Labradoodle?" or "What kind of poodle is that?", I'd be a rich man. It's got to the point where the elaborate naming of this wonderful, curious, gregarious animal almost sticks in my craw. Murray River Curly Coated Retriever. Five, long-feeling words. People often think I am joking.

History doesn't serve the dogs well; scant information is offered about their inception, but lore says the landrace breed came about likely from Norfolk Retrievers or American Water Spaniels, though there's confusion with Chesapeake Bay Retrievers, Curly Coated Retrievers and tenuous links to English Springer Spaniels and Irish Water Spaniels.

Function of the animals dictated form; during the early days of the paddle steamers chugging up and down the Murray, you'd have likely found the zigging and zagging of liver-coloured, ringlet-haired, golden-eyed dogs as they bounded up and down the gangplanks of the paddle steamers. Steady of foot on duck punts, instinctive in retrieval of their quarry, webbing between toes for easy gait in water. They were meant for life on the Murray.

The Murray River Curly Coated Retriever is arguably Australia's first dog of terroir. While a rare breed scattered across Australia, the dogs continue to be endemic around the Murray River in Victoria, South Australia and southern New South Wales. Krumpli herself came from Rushworth in Victoria, just southeast of the famed Murray River town of Echuca where the paddle steamers once thumped at the water with regularity.

Even now, as I peer over sepia-toned photographs of the old Murray River with their parasol-clutching women, well-dressed, moustachioed-and-top-hat-resplendent men, I get a sense of nostalgia and history that drags me back to my few visits to quiet corners of Australia's largest river. My dog continues the reminder.

All dogs come from somewhere. And all dogs would have originally emerged from a local culture or region, intrinsically linked to the customs, behaviours and environment from which they were born. Australia has the native dingo as its original canine totem, but it also has the Murray River Curly Coated Retriever – a dog that gives you a sense, like the concept of terroir in winemaking, of humankind's intervention coupled to heritage and place.

MIKE BENNIE IS ONE OF AUSTRALIA'S FOREMOST WINE WRITERS AND PRESENTERS AND IS A FEATURE WRITER FOR *GOURMET TRAVELLER WINE* MAGAZINE, EDITOR-AT-LARGE OF THE HIGHLY RESPECTED INDUSTRY WEBSITE WINEFRONT.COM.AU AND WINE/DRINKS EDITOR FOR *DELICIOUS* MAGAZINE. MIKE IS ALSO A LOCAL AND INTERNATIONAL WINE JUDGE. HIS WORK HAS APPEARED IN *TIME OUT*, THE *SUNDAY TELEGRAPH STYLE* MAGAZINE AND *MEN'S STYLE*, AND MANY OTHER PUBLICATIONS. HE LIKES LONG WALKS ON THE BEACH WITH A BOTTLE OF WINE IN HAND.

MOLLY

PET HATE: CHEFS
OWNER: NICK BROWN
OBSESSION: CHASING BIRDS
NAUGHTIEST DEED: DESTROYING THE OUTDOOR
FURNITURE WHEN LEFT AT HOME BY HERSELF
FAVOURITE TOYS: THE FORKLIFT AND TENNIS BALLS
FAVOURITE PASTIME: RIDING ON THE BACK OF THE UTE
KNOWN ACCOMPLICE: BARRY, THE ALL SAINTS MAINTENANCE SUPERVISOR

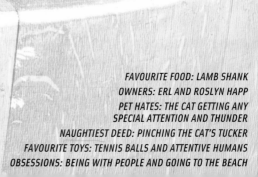

FAVOURITE FOOD: LAMB SHANK
OWNERS: ERL AND ROSLYN HAPP
PET HATES: THE CAT GETTING ANY
SPECIAL ATTENTION AND THUNDER
NAUGHTIEST DEED: PINCHING THE CAT'S TUCKER
FAVOURITE TOYS: TENNIS BALLS AND ATTENTIVE HUMANS
OBSESSIONS: BEING WITH PEOPLE AND GOING TO THE BEACH

JEDDA

RED

OBSESSION: ESCAPOLOGY
KNOWN ACCOMPLICE: LARA
NAUGHTIEST DEED: HELPING HIMSELF
TO THE SMOKED PIG'S EAR IN THE PET SHOP
OWNERS: JENNY AND GRAHAM ELLENDER
PET HATE: NOT GOING IN THE UTE WITH GRAHAM
FAVOURITE PASTIME: BEING PETTED BY WINERY VISITORS

FAVOURITE FOOD: APPLES
FAVOURITE TOY: POLYPIPE OFF-CUTS
OBSESSION: ESCAPOLOGY WITH RED
NAUGHTIEST DEED: CHEWING THROUGH
THE VACUUM CLEANER POWER CABLE
OWNERS: JENNY AND GRAHAM ELLENDER
FAVOURITE PASTIME: COMPETING WITH RED FOR
WINERY VISITORS' ATTENTION BY FALLING OVER

NELLE

Huntington

PET HATES: CROWS AND MAGPIES
OWNERS: TIM AND NICKY STEVENS
KNOWN ACCOMPLICE: DIEGO FROM
MUDGEE HOMESTEAD GUEST HOUSE
OBSESSION: BRAD THE VINEYARD HAND
FAVOURITE FOOD: SPAGHETTI BOLOGNESE
FAVOURITE TOY: BRAD THE VINEYARD HAND

TOBY

PET HATE: BIRDS
OWNER: RICHARD WELLSMORE
FAVOURITE TOY: ANYTHING CHASABLE
FAVOURITE PASTIME: PLAYING TUG-OF-WAR
NAUGHTIEST DEEDS: CHASING CHICKENS AND SNEAKING INSIDE
KNOWN ACCOMPLICE: ANY DOG THAT WILL HELP HIM CHASE CHICKENS
OBSESSIONS: CHASING RABBITS AND CHICKENS AND SNEAKING INSIDE

TAZ

PHOEBE

ARCHIMEDES

FAVOURITE TOY: BALLS
PET HATE: HAVING BATHS
NAUGHTIEST DEED: ESCAPING
OBSESSION: PLAYING WITH BALLS
OWNERS: CONOR AND HEIDI VAN DER REEST
FAVOURITE PASTIME: PLAYING FETCH WITH HER BALL

FAVOURITE TOY: BONES
NAUGHTIEST DEED: ESCAPING
OBSESSION: BEING CLOSE TO HIS OWNERS
PET HATE: BEING LOCKED UP IN THE KENNEL
OWNERS: CONOR AND HEIDI VAN DER REEST
FAVOURITE PASTIMES: GETTING PATS AND PLAYING CHASE

BUSTER

KOONARA
COONAWARRA

OWNER: DRU RESCHKE

PET HATE: THE WORD "BATH"

FAVOURITE TOY: DRU'S SOCKS

OBSESSION: TRICKS FOR TREATS

NAUGHTIEST DEED: WEEING ON A
CUSTOMER'S FOOT WHEN HE WAS A PUPPY

FAVOURITE PASTIME: DOING HIS RANGE OF TRICKS FOR VISITORS

PET HATE: *LOUD NOISES*
FAVOURITE PASTIME: *SWIMMING*
OBSESSIONS: *OCEANS AND DAMS*
OWNERS: *CHRIS, JO AND LUCAS DAVIES*
NAUGHTIEST DEED: *CHASING BIRDS IN THE VINE NETS*

MR BEAR

INDI

FOOD: PIG'S EARS
OWNERS: TANYA AND MICHAEL OLINDER
PET HATES: CORKS POPPING AND MICROWAVES
FAVOURITE TOY: GRANDMA'S GARDENING SHOES
NAUGHTIEST DEED: RUNNING INTO A FAMOUS
CHEESE SHOP IN TASSIE AND PEEING ON THE FLOOR
FAVOURITE PASTIME: GOING DOWN SLIPPERY SLIDES

LILA

PET HATE: COMING BACK WHEN CALLED
OWNERS: TANYA AND MICHAEL OLINDER
OBSESSION: GREETING EVERYONE SHE SEES
FAVOURITE TOY: GRANDMA'S HOSE FITTINGS
FAVOURITE FOOD: TIGGER THE CAT'S DINNER
FAVOURITE PASTIME: ROLLING IN SMELLY THINGS
NAUGHTIEST DEED: CHEWING A LEXUS' LEATHER DOOR TRIM

FAVOURITE TOY: STICKS
OBSESSION: TUMMY RUBS
PET HATE: HAVING A BATH
FAVOURITE FOODS: STEAK AND PASTA
FAVOURITE PASTIME: CHASING HIS
MUM KONNIE AROUND THE PROPERTY
NAUGHTIEST DEED: CHASING CHICKENS
OWNERS: BILL WHALLEY AND JANE McLEAN

KYUS

FAVOURITE FOODS: CHICKEN AND RICE
OBSESSION: EXPLORING THE PROPERTY
FAVOURITE TOYS: STONES (TO CHEW ON)
OWNERS: BILL WHALLEY AND JANE McLEAN
PET HATE: HAVING HER EARS BLOW-DRIED
FAVOURITE PASTIME: SWIMMING IN THE DAM
NAUGHTIEST DEED: PULLING THE ROOSTER'S TAIL

KAIA

COCO

OWNERS: GABRIELA AND BARRY WHITE
FAVOURITE FOODS: SALMON AND MILLIPEDES
FAVOURITE PASTIME: LOOKING INNOCENT BUT BEING A DEVIL
OBSESSION: ANYTHING THAT CAN BE CHEWED, GNAWED, BROKEN OR TORN
NAUGHTIEST DEED: TRASHING WEDDING DECORATIONS JUST BEFORE THE EVENT

OBSESSION: FOOD
OWNERS: GABRIELA AND BARRY WHITE
FAVOURITE PASTIMES: EATING AND SNORING
KNOWN ACCOMPLICE: COCO THE TROUBLEMAKER
NAUGHTIEST DEED: RAIDING BARRY'S SUNDAY BBQ MEAT TRAYS

RUBY

NERO

FAVOURITE TOY: OLD BONES
FAVOURITE FOOD: CASSEROLE
OBSESSION: FOOD GLORIOUS FOOD
FAVOURITE PASTIME: CHEWING A BONE
PET HATE: SOMEONE BLOWING IN HIS EAR
OWNERS: MARC DOBSON AND LARRY JACOBS
NAUGHTIEST DEED: EXCAVATING BURIED COWS

FAVOURITE FOOD: *LAMB FAT*
OBSESSION: *HERDING THE UTE*
FAVOURITE TOYS: *VINEYARD STICK AND BALL*
OWNERS: *MARC DOBSON AND LARRY JACOBS*
NAUGHTIEST DEED: *STEALING THE NEIGHBOUR'S TRAINERS*
FAVOURITE PASTIME: *GREETING VISITORS AT THE CELLAR DOOR*
PET HATES: *THUNDERSTORMS AND THINGS THAT GO BUMP IN THE NIGHT*

BACCHUS

FAVOURITE TOY: FRISBEE
PET HATE: BEING YELLED AT
OWNERS: BRIAN AND ROS LYNN
NAUGHTIEST DEED: CHASING TRUCKS
FAVOURITE PASTIME: PLAYING WITH STICKS
OBSESSION: ANYTHING HE CAN DROP AT YOUR FEET

CARL

ROSIE

FAVOURITE TOY: STUFFED FROG
OWNERS: MARK AND ANNETTE BARRY
NAUGHTIEST DEED: HIDING UNDER THE TABLE
WHEN IT'S TIME TO GO TO BED IN THE LAUNDRY
OBSESSION: LICKING PEOPLE'S ARMS AND LEGS
FAVOURITE PASTIME: ROLLING OVER FOR PEOPLE TO PAT HER
FAVOURITE FOOD: CHEESE AND CRACKERS FROM CELLAR DOOR

CHESTER

FAVOURITE TOY: ROSIE
OWNERS: MARK AND ANNETTE BARRY
FAVOURITE PASTIME: CHASING RABBITS
OBSESSION: GREETING CELLAR DOOR CUSTOMERS
FAVOURITE FOOD: ANYTHING OFF SOMEONE'S PLATE
PET HATE: BEING WASHED IN THE LAUNDRY TROUGH
NAUGHTIEST DEED: COCKING HIS LEG ON THE WINERY BLACKBOARDS

JUNO

OWNER: CHARLES WHISH
PET HATE: BEING LEFT BEHIND
FAVOURITE PASTIMES: VISITING
THE VINEYARD AND CHASING BALLS
FAVOURITE FOOD: MARROWBONES
OBSESSION: PLASTIC SQUEAKY CHOOK
NAUGHTIEST DEED: EATING A MOTHER'S
DAY CAKE STRAIGHT OUT OF THE OVEN

TREVOR

ALIAS: THE TREVORNATOR
OBSESSION: PLAYING CRICKET
ON THE BEACH (UNINVITED)
FAVOURITE TOY: SQUEAKY CHICKEN
OWNERS: DAVID PAXTON AND ANG TOLLEY
FAVOURITE PASTIME: RIDING IN ANY AVAILABLE
CAR WITH HIS HEAD OUT THE WINDOW
NAUGHTIEST DEED: SHARING NEIGHBOURS' BBQS

ROCCO

PET HATE: LOUD NOISES
NAUGHTIEST DEED: STEALING
STEAK FROM SHOPPING BAGS
FAVOURITE FOOD: MINCEMEAT
FAVOURITE TOYS: STICKS, TWIGS AND BARK
OWNERS: DAVID PAXTON AND ANG TOLLEY
FAVOURITE PASTIME: BEING A MUMMY'S
BOY AND GETTING ATTENTION

MILLY

OBSESSION: MAGPIES
FAVOURITE FOOD: CHICKEN
FAVOURITE PASTIME: EATING
OWNER: SAN PENFOLD HYLAND
FAVOURITE TOY: OLD TEDDY BEAR
PET HATE: HAVING HER TOENAILS TRIMMED

BANJO

FAVOURITE FOOD: HAM
KNOWN ACCOMPLICE: FINN
OWNERS: HELEN AND JOHN EDWARDS
FAVOURITE PASTIME: SHADOWING HELEN
OBSESSION: OBSESSION? A BORDER COLLIE! NEVER!
FAVOURITE TOYS: TWO CHOOKS CALLED HENNY AND PENNY
NAUGHTIEST DEED: FORGETTING NOT TO JUMP UP ON VISITORS

PET HATE: FOXES
OWNERS: DAVE AND DIANA PALMER
FAVOURITE PASTIME: SLEEPING IN THE SUN
OBSESSION: FOLLOWING DAVE EVERYWHERE
FAVOURITE FOOD: SANDWICHES FROM THE WINERY STAFF
NAUGHTIEST DEED: RIPPING UP UNATTENDED RUBBISH BAG

MAX

"When an eighty-five pound mammal
licks your tears away, then tries to
sit on your lap, it's hard to feel sad."

KRISTAN HIGGINS

SCRATCHING the BLACK DOG

by Tory Shepherd

IF YOU'RE EVER FEELING a bit sorry for yourself, Google "two-legged dog".

There's one guy, Duncan Lou Who. He's a Boxer who had his two hind legs amputated after a birth defect. He has wheelchairs, but prefers to toddle along on those two legs, his tongue hanging out and his torso bumping along behind him. It would be comical if it wasn't so damn uplifting to see him trot along like that. There is a YouTube video of Duncan gallivanting along a beach. Half a dog, with his tail wagging above empty space, going like the clappers.

Diesel's a Border cross Kelpie from Stepney in Adelaide. He lost a leg in a car accident. It was distressing, tragic. He survived and his family, Bear and Georgie, wondered how he'd cope. Diesel, now? Full of fuel. Enough to keep up with the family additions, Chloe and Ella. One of his best tricks is when he goes to the toilet. He doesn't cock the nonexistent leg. He lifts the other one. Which effectively leaves him doing a handstand to mark his territory. It is both noble and hilarious.

Then there's Stella. A startlingly intense dog who survived the bushfires that tore through the Adelaide Hills in early 2015. Her furless parents, Sarah and Ben, will never know exactly what she went through when the kennels she was staying in were hit. It was a terrible, chaotic time.

For hours they didn't know if she was alive or dead. The community there – pretty towns framed by vineyards and orchards, where the local pub is the beating heart – kept hearing different stories. Roads were closed, there was no electricity, and too much wrong information. Lots of animals didn't make it.

But then for them, a beautiful moment. The local newspaper, my newspaper *The Advertiser*, published a picture online of a dusty firefighter emerging from the smoke – with Stella. Sarah and Ben thought she'd be traumatised, this survivor from the horror. But all she wanted was a scratch under her red bandanna and a run at the beach. Stella's just fine.

That's the thing about dogs. They only get screwed up in the head if humans make them that way through breeding or neglect or abuse. They're resilient.

Humans, on the other hand, screw themselves up in the head for no good reason. We struggle to find happiness even when we have all our legs, and can go to the toilet in a civilised way, and haven't even had an inferno pass over our heads.

We're not happy, even when someone keeps taking us to the beach or throwing the ball for us. We always want more.

Except, often, when we're around dogs. Dogs (OK, dogs and wine) are the best therapy. These slobbery creatures, these farty furballs, are the ones who help us get a better grip on our lives. In return for artificial beef-flavoured brown balls, day after day, they give us back happiness.

Next time you're feeling a bit crap, think about what it would be like to get around with one leg, or to be stuck in the smoke not knowing where your family is. And if that doesn't put your troubles in perspective, just go scratch a dog behind the ear.

You'll feel better, I promise.

TORY SHEPHERD IS THE POLITICAL EDITOR AT *THE ADVERTISER* AND SPLITS HER TIME BETWEEN ADELAIDE AND CANBERRA. SHE IS LUCKY ENOUGH TO HAVE FRIENDS WHO SEND HER FUNNY DOG PICTURES OR TAKE HER OUT FOR WINE WHENEVER SHE'S HAD ENOUGH OF THE NATION'S POLITICIANS.

ANGAS

PET HATE: BIRDS

OWNER: HAMISH MAGUIRE

FAVOURITE FOOD: DUCK LIVER PARFAIT
WITH TRUFFLE BUTTER, GRILLED BRIOCHE
AND SERVED WITH POACHED PEAR

OBSESSION: CLASSIC LITERATURE (SCOOBY
DOO, SNOOPY – MAINLY HIS EARLY WORK)

FAVOURITE PASTIME: BEING AN ENVIRONMENTALIST
(ALL COMPOSTABLE MATERIAL MUST BE THOROUGHLY REVIEWED)

OWNER: MICHAEL SAWYER
NAUGHTIEST DEED: BRINGING IN AND EATING
MUDDY BONES ON NEW CARPET WHILE MICHAEL
IS IN THE SHOWER (IN TWO DIFFERENT HOUSES)
PET HATES: BEING BRUSHED AND NEXT DOOR'S CAT
FAVOURITE TOY: AN EMPTY GARDEN POT HE PUTS HIS
HEAD IN AND PUSHES AROUND THE GARDEN ALL DAY
FAVOURITE FOODS: CHEESE, BANANAS AND FILLET STEAK

TOBY

OSCAR

OWNERS: CATE AND COLIN ARNOLD
FAVOURITE FOODS: CELLAR DOOR
LEFTOVERS AND MARROWBONES
OBSESSION: CHASING RABBITS AND MAGPIES
FAVOURITE PASTIME: RIDING IN THE FLAT TRAY
NAUGHTIEST DEED: THE 'NATIVE HEN INCIDENT'
FAVOURITE TOYS: GARDENING GLOVES AND HIS LEAD
PET HATE: NOT BEING ALLOWED TO RIDE IN THE FLAT TRAY

PEBBLES

FAVOURITE TOY: OSCAR
OBSESSION: LICKING BABIES
FAVOURITE FOOD: LEFTOVERS
OWNERS: CATE AND COLIN ARNOLD
FAVOURITE PASTIMES: VINEYARD WALKS
AND SLEEPING OUTSIDE CELLAR DOOR
NAUGHTIEST DEEDS: BOSSING OSCAR
AROUND AND 'THE PLOVER INCIDENT'
PET HATES: FLIES AND BEING LEFT BEHIND

FAVOURITE TOY: OLD SHERRIN FOOTY
PET HATES: THUNDER AND LIGHTNING
OWNERS: LUKE AND MADELINE SKEER
FAVOURITE FOOD: LOCAL LAMB CHOPS
OBSESSIONS: CHASING BALLS AND SWIMMING AT THE BEACH
FAVOURITE PASTIMES: MORNING RUNS AND ROUGH PLAY WITH OLIVER
NAUGHTIEST DEED: SNEAKING INTO THE VINEYARD TO EAT RIPE CABERNET GRAPES

ZEUS

MANA

FAVOURITE TOY: FROGGY
FAVOURITE FOOD: CHICKENS
PET HATE: BEING LEFT BEHIND
OBSESSION: CHASING SMALL ANIMALS
FAVOURITE PASTIME: CHASING RABBITS
OWNERS: CRAIG VINEY AND RUBY STOBART
NAUGHTIEST DEED: EATING THE NEIGHBOUR'S CHICKENS

TASH

PET HATE: WATER
FAVOURITE FOOD: CAT FOOD
FAVOURITE TOYS: STICKS AND ODD SOCKS
OBSESSION: TAKING FLUFF OUT OF PILLOWS
FAVOURITE PASTIME: SLEEPING IN THE SUN
NAUGHTIEST DEED: CHEWING THE TV REMOTE
OWNERS: ANDREW, VANESSA, ALEC AND OSCAR SEPPELT

COOPER

FAVOURITE TOY: UTE TYRES
OBSESSION: THE WINERY UTE
PET HATE: BEING LEFT BEHIND
FAVOURITE PASTIME: CHASING BIRDS
FAVOURITE FOOD: ROAST LAMB BONES
NAUGHTIEST DEED: TAKING HIMSELF TO THE PUB
OWNERS: ANDREW, VANESSA, ALEC AND OSCAR SEPPELT

RAFFI

OWNER: CLAIRE TONON
FAVOURITE TOY: HIS HOTDOG
FAVOURITE FOOD: ANYTHING CLAIRE'S EATING
FAVOURITE PASTIME: WALKING WITH HIS HOTDOG
OBSESSION: SLEEPING NEXT TO, IF NOT ON TOP OF, CLAIRE
NAUGHTIEST DEED: ROLLING AROUND IN FRESH SHEEP MANURE

PET HATE: BATHS
FAVOURITE PASTIME:
LONG WEEKEND WALKS
OWNER: SANDY THOMAS
OBSESSION: DAD'S BEEF JERKY
FAVOURITE TOY: BABE THE PIG
NAUGHTIEST DEED: EATING DAD'S
CHEESE KRANSKY AND LEAVING THE
PAPER BAG AS IF IT WAS UNTOUCHED

FENG-SHUI

MADDIE

OBSESSION: PUPPIES
OWNERS: PETER AND ROZ SEPPELT
FAVOURITE FOOD: MARROWBONES
FAVOURITE TOY: EVERYBODY ELSE'S BONES
FAVOURITE PASTIME: LOOKING AFTER HER PUPPIES

FAVOURITE FOOD: FIGS
FAVOURITE TOY: LEAVES
OWNERS: PETER AND ROZ SEPPELT
OBSESSION: MOOCHING FOR PIZZA
FAVOURITE PASTIME: VISITING THE 'OLDIES' AT AGED CARE

MALT

PET HATE: CATS
OWNER: ROZ SEPPELT
FAVOURITE FOOD: PIZZA
FAVOURITE TOY: THE QUAD BIKE
NAUGHTIEST DEED: ROLLING IN SOMETHING
DEAD ON ROZ AND PETER'S WEDDING DAY
OBSESSION: PLAYING SOCCER WITH VISITORS
FAVOURITE PASTIME: WATCHING THE HORSES

BELLA

PET HATE: WAKING UP
FAVOURITE TOY: HIS BED
FAVOURITE PASTIME: SLEEPING
OWNERS: PETER AND ROZ SEPPELT
NAUGHTIEST DEED: NOT WAKING UP
OBSESSION: SLEEPING IN FRONT OF THE FIRE

TOBY

ARCHIE

FAVOURITE TOY: DONKEY
OBSESSIONS: RABBITS AND WALKIES
OWNERS: PAUL BRIDGEMAN AND CAROLINE MOONEY
FAVOURITE PASTIME: MEET N' GREET WITH THE VISITORS
PET HATES: HIS IBS DIET AND HAVING HIS REST DISTURBED
NAUGHTIEST DEED: PUTTING MUDDY PAWS ON PRISTINE WHITE PANTS

Caesar's Paddock
Perigord Truffles

OWNER: COLLEEN JREISSATI
OBSESSION: HIS PERSONAL TREAT
BAG WHICH HE CARRIES EVERYWHERE
PET HATE: THE HUMAN INABILITY TO
COMPREHEND HIS SENSE OF SUPERIORITY
FAVOURITE FOOD: MEDIUM RARE WAGYU BEEF
WITH SHAVINGS OF PERIGORD TRUFFLES
NAUGHTIEST DEED: DIGGING HOLES IN THE DIRT
AND CURLING UP IN THEM STRAIGHT AFTER A BATH

CAESAR

SAM

PET HATE: CATS
OWNER: STUART PITTS
FAVOURITE PASTIME: SWIMMING
FAVOURITE TOY: THE SOCCER BALL
NAUGHTIEST DEED: CHASING CATS
OBSESSION: KICKING THE SOCCER BALL

OWNER: VIRGINIA WILLCOCK
PET HATES: BANGS, CRASHES AND MOTORS
FAVOURITE PASTIME: HANGING WITH VIRGINIA
NAUGHTIEST DEED: RIPPING APART CUSHIONS
WITH AUSTIN AND SLEEPING IN A PILE OF FLUFF
OBSESSION: HIS FLUFFY BIG COUSIN AUSTIN, THE LABRADOR

IAIN

OBSESSION: SUNSHINE
PET HATE: BEING ALONE
FAVOURITE TOY: THE ODD DEAD RABBIT
OWNERS: FIONA WELLER AND JULIAN ALLPORT
FAVOURITE FOOD: TASMANIAN ARTISANAL CHEESE
NAUGHTIEST DEED: STEALING THE CHRISTMAS HAM
FAVOURITE PASTIME: GETTING CUDDLES FROM VISITORS

OTTO

OBSESSION: LICKING EARS
OWNERS: KYM AND VANESSA TEUSNER
FAVOURITE PASTIMES: SWIMMING IN THE
VINEYARD DAMS AND PLAYING TUG OF WAR
NAUGHTIEST DEED: HOUDINI-LIKE ESCAPES
FAVOURITE FOOD: EVERYTHING, INCLUDING DYNAMIC LIFTER
PET HATE: BEING LEFT OUTSIDE THE POOL YARD WHEN THE FAMILY IS SWIMMING

ASLAN

BOB THE DOG

FAVOURITE TOY: RED BALL
FAVOURITE FOOD: FRESH RABBIT
OBSESSIONS: BUNGS AND WARWICK
PET HATE: THE VET'S FINGER PROBE
OWNERS: WARWICK MURRAY AND CHAI-HUA LOKE
NAUGHTIEST DEED: BEING A PUPPY SCHOOL DROPOUT
FAVOURITE PASTIMES: GOING TO WORK ON THE UTE AND WALKING TO THE PUB

OWNER: MICK PAGE
OBSESSION: LICKING EVERYONE
FAVOURITE FOOD: ANYTHING LEFT
UNATTENDED ON THE LUNCH TABLE
NAUGHTIEST DEED: WELCOMING ALL
VISITORS WITH A NOSE TO THE CROTCH
FAVOURITE PASTIME: CAMPING ON THE RIVER
PET HATES: TRAILERS AND NOT GOING TO WORK

COOPER

COCO

OWNERS: JUDY AND GLEN KELLY
NAUGHTIEST DEED: STEALING
A PURSE FROM A CUSTOMER'S BAG
FAVOURITE PASTIMES: RIDING IN THE
CAR WITH JUDY AND WATCHING TV
PET HATES: WINDSCREEN WIPERS AND STORMS
FAVOURITE FOODS: CHEESE AND PEANUT BUTTER
OBSESSIONS: JUDY AND STEALING GLEN'S SOCKS

KNOWN ACCOMPLICE: WOLFIE
OWNERS: THE LUBIANA FAMILY
PET HATE: BEING WITHOUT STEVE
NAUGHTIEST DEED: EATING THE COMPOST
OBSESSION: FOLLOWING STEVE EVERYWHERE
FAVOURITE PASTIME: MOUSE-HUNTING IN THE VINEYARD

JAFFA

KELPIE, 5 | **STEFANO LUBIANA WINES** GRANTON, TAS | 93

FAVOURITE PASTIME: LYING
ON HER BACK AND BEING PATTED
FAVOURITE TOYS: HUMANS WITH FOOD
OWNERS: DARREN AND JACKIE BROWN
NAUGHTIEST DEED: EATING ROTTEN DUCK EGGS
THEN PASSING GAS IN THE CELLAR DOOR
PET HATE: LUCKY DUCK GETTING MORE PATS THAN HER
FAVOURITE FOOD: ANYTHING EXCEPT PEAS AND CARROTS

FAVOURITE FOOD: WHEAT
FAVOURITE PASTIMES: PADDLING
IN THE POND AND HAVING CUDDLES
OWNERS: DARREN AND JACKIE BROWN
PET HATE: SHARING THE WHEAT BUCKET
FAVOURITE TOYS: PAINTED TOES AND 'BLING'
OBSESSION: BEING TOP DOG (OR IS THAT 'TOP DUCK'?)
NAUGHTIEST DEED: POOING ON HANDS, ARMS, FEET, FLOORS...

OWNER: MATT CALDERSMITH
PET HATE: WAVES AT THE BEACH
FAVOURITE FOOD: CHICKEN NECKS
FAVOURITE TOY: A FLAT RAT SQUEAKY TOY
OBSESSIONS: FOOD AND BELLY SCRATCHES
FAVOURITE PASTIMES: CHASING ALVIN THE CAT AND STEALING WORK BOOTS
NAUGHTIEST DEED: JUMPING STACKED PACKING BOXES TO EAT ALVIN'S FOOD

CHEWBACCA

ZAC

PET HATE: BEING LEFT HOME
OWNERS: GREG AND ALLISON HOBBS
FAVOURITE FOOD: FRESHLY CAUGHT RABBIT
FAVOURITE TOYS: ANY SINGLE SOCK OR SHOE
OBSESSION: CHASING RABBITS IN THE BACKYARD
FAVOURITE PASTIME: PAYING 'ROCK STAR' VISITS TO THE ARTISANS CELLAR DOOR
NAUGHTIEST DEED: STEALING SHOES AND DROPPING THEM SOMEWHERE OUTSIDE

OWNER: MARY HAMILTON
PET HATE: BEING LEFT BEHIND
NAUGHTIEST DEED: CONFUSING SNAIL BAIT FOR A TASTY SNACK
OBSESSIONS: FOOD, MARY AND RETRIEVING BALLS FROM THE SEA
FAVOURITE PASTIME: CASING OUT PLAYGROUNDS FOR DROPPED SANDWICHES
FAVOURITE TOY: ONE THAT HE CAN UNWRAP HIMSELF AND DEMOLISH IN TEN MINUTES

HORACE

JUDAH

OBSESSION: EATING
OWNER: WENDY COUPE
FAVOURITE TOY: TEDDY BEAR
FAVOURITE PASTIME: EATING
PET HATES: THUNDER AND FIRE CRACKERS
NAUGHTIEST DEED: EATING THE STRAWBERRIES
AND SNOW PEAS FROM THE VEGETABLE GARDEN

PET HATE: PINOT D PIG
FAVOURITE FOOD: RABBITS
OBSESSION: BARREL BUNGS
OWNERS: TIM AND BEC DUFFY
NAUGHTIEST DEED: STEALING BUNGS
FAVOURITE PASTIME: SWIMMING IN THE TAMAR RIVER
KNOWN ACCOMPLICES: PINOT D PIG AND FINNEGAN THE KELPIE

BELLA

"Every once in a while,
a dog enters your life
and changes everything."

ANONYMOUS

EDELWEISS ERNIE

by Ben Canaider

MY MOTHER HAS ALWAYS BEEN
a great exponent of the pathetic fallacy. That's the
notion of ascribing human emotions to things which
aren't human, like rocks or clouds or animals. She
is brilliant at it, and believes that if animals can
have human feelings they should be treated like
humans. Hard hearts, cruel hearts, don't believe in
this emotional nonsense. Of course not. Everyone
reading this book, however, would be a dead-set
believer in the pathetic fallacy idea.

It can be taken to extremes, though, as I discovered
when I turned 12, and when Mum brought home
a posh, pedigreed German Shepherd. Ernie.
Edelweiss Ernie, as his kennel warranty put it.

He was a fabulously handsome if somewhat shaky
puppy. Not uncoordinated like big dogs in their
puppy form can be; but shaky as in traumatised.
He'd recently been shot at. The shot missed, but
Ernie was left unhinged. His kennel owner had sold
Ernie but the cheque had bounced. The kennel owner
went around to the bouncee's farm to shoot the dog.
BANG. A fight followed, the police came, and so on
and so forth.

My mother did goody-goody pro bono work for a
dog charity. She was invariably the person they
called when they had an unhinged dog. We'd
had plenty of such dogs during my childhood.
There was an Afghan Hound (Demis – named
after Demis Roussos... don't ask me why...)
who only wanted to run in a straight line.

There was Lurch the Weimaraner who had to howl
(or sing, as Mum put it). And there was also a black
Labrador who thought she was one of the Bronte
sisters reincarnated – Emily. Golly, she was a tragic.
Kept trying to drown herself. But Ernie was the pick of
them, and had the greatest effect on my young life.

Because Ernie now became my equal. Or, perhaps,
I became his equal. My mother's reckless indulgence
for me was now split in two. Half for me, and half for
Ernie. Sometimes though, it felt more like 40/60 –
and definitely in the dog's favour.

Our – the family's – diet changed. Car travel changed.
Everything changed. All thanks to Ernie. My mother
started to cook again. But for Ernie. She made him
wonderful beef stews, and chicken dishes. Lots of
couscous and sausage. Rice dishes. Dad and
I ate like horses, living on alfalfa sprouts.

The front passenger seat was taken out of the Volkswagen so that Ernie could sit more easily – riding up the front with his mother. I sat on the back seat, without a window to wind down…

Weekends centred around Ernie's exercise and leisure regime. Mum and Dad would drive him off to staggeringly impressive bits of our mountain-top geography so he could prance about like a prince of a German duchy. This meant I had to walk to everything. Football. Friends. Fun. All on foot. Oh, did I mention we lived in the mountains?

If I had a sore tooth I was told it was a growing pain. If Ernie looked in anything less than picture-postcard condition, then he'd be rushed to the vet by medi-vac air-ambulance. Being my mother's son, though, I couldn't defeat the gene. There was something about Ernie. And I came to love him. I tried to not let it show.

And this is how my adolescence went. Hours became days and days turned into weeks and in and out of years until I got home from university one day and saw a sign posted on the laundry door – or Ernie's room. "Do not disturb. Ernie is depressed."

I opened the door. He was on his day bed, with his jaw resting on his crossed-over front paws.

His eyes were sort of milky, and he didn't even look up at me – not a glance. Not a jot of the sort of brotherly look he'd been giving me for eight years. "Hi Ben, you're home, do you want to run around out the back for a bit?"

Ernie was depressed. He was 8. His back legs had recently been a bit wobbly. Early stages of dog arthritis, his medical team had diagnosed. Had he seen the writing on the wall? If you can't be 100% German Shepherd why bother being a German Shepherd at all? Why bother living?

If you can't climb into your customised German car and be chauffeured around to impressive bits of mountain top where you can do canine impersonations of Ludwig II at exercise, why go on?

Ernie died a few weeks later. There were some other health issues, it proved. He died, I moved out of home, my mother seem to strangely age. My father kept putting acres of alfalfa shoots into his cheese sandwiches. He'd come to quite like the stuff. Or maybe he was remembering Ernie.

They got another dog about a year later, but it only ever barked at me, as if I were a complete stranger. It was just a dog. But my brother had been a German Shepherd.

BEN CANAIDER IS A WINE AND DRINKS WRITER AND AUTHOR. HE IS PUBLISHED IN BOTH EUROPE AND THE USA, AND IN FOUR LANGUAGES. HE NEVER DINES IN RESTAURANTS HE HASN'T BEEN TO BEFORE.
THIS STORY HAS BEEN REPRINTED FROM *WINE DOGS AUSTRALIA 3*, PUBLISHED 2012.

OWNER: JIM CHATTO
PET HATE: CAUSTIC ON THE FLOOR
OBSESSION: THE MIGHTY BOMBERS
FAVOURITE FOOD: GROWN-UP FOOD
FAVOURITE PASTIME: GOING TO WORK
NAUGHTIEST DEED: MARKING HIS TERRITORY
IN THE HALLOWED O'SHEA ROOM

GARY

HONOUR

NAUGHTIEST DEED:
CATCHING A RABBIT
PET HATE: NOT LIVING INSIDE
OWNER: CHRISTINE McKINLEY
FAVOURITE PASTIME:
MAINTAINING HER GIRLISH
FIGURE BY GOING ON LONG WALKS
OBSESSION: MEETING PEOPLE

PET HATE: *BEING ALONE*
OWNER: *CHRISTINE McKINLEY*
FAVOURITE TOY: *ANYTHING THAT SQUEAKS*
FAVOURITE FOODS: *RAW CHICKEN NECKS AND WINGS*
OBSESSION: *PLAYING WITH BROTHERS COHEN AND KYE*
NAUGHTIEST DEED: *DRAGGING BEDDING OUT INTO THE RAIN*

LEXI

BILLIE

OWNER: CHARLIE O'BRIEN
PET HATE: VACUUM CLEANER
FAVOURITE FOOD: FRESH FISH
OBSESSION: BEING ON KANGAROO WATCH
FAVOURITE PASTIMES: SNOOZING AND HAVING CUDDLES
NAUGHTIEST DEED: RELEASING DANGEROUS GASES INTO THE ATMOSPHERE

SEMILLON

CHARDONNAY

FAVOURITE TOY: KONG ON A ROPE
OBSESSIONS: FOOD AND SWIMMING
PET HATES: BATHTIME AND CAR RIDES
NAUGHTIEST DEED: ROLLING IN COW POO
OWNERS: VICCI LASHMORE-SMITH AND ERIC SMITH
FAVOURITE FOOD: EVERYTHING INCLUDING KANGAROO POO
FAVOURITE PASTIME: PLAYING WITH PEOPLE AT CELLAR DOOR

FAVOURITE TOY: FLUFFY DUCK
PET HATE: VICCI GOING OUT WITHOUT HER
FAVOURITE FOOD: PARTIAL TO A NIP OF WHISKY
OBSESSION: SLEEPING ON VICCI AND ERIC'S BED
OWNERS: VICCI LASHMORE-SMITH AND ERIC SMITH
NAUGHTIEST DEED: CHEWING THE CAT FLAP OUT OF THE DOOR
FAVOURITE PASTIMES: SWIMMING IN THE DAM AND SLEEPING

FAVOURITE TOY: SOFT CUSHIONS
OBSESSION: WATCHING TELEVISION
PET HATE: DOGS ON HER TELEVISION
NAUGHTIEST DEED: POOING ON PATHWAYS
OWNERS: JULIE BARRY AND BEN JEANNERET
FAVOURITE PASTIME: CHASING HER FAVOURITE
FRIENDS, JASPER, OSCAR AND DULCIE BELLE

MINI

OWNER: JUSTIN PURSER
FAVOURITE TOY: HALF-ROTTEN FURRY DUCK TOY
FAVOURITE PASTIME: GOING FOR RUNS AROUND
THE VINEYARDS AND CHASING ANY RABBITS,
MAGPIES OR SMALL CHILDREN ALONG THE WAY
FAVOURITE FOODS: LAMB BONES, PIG'S EARS AND STINKY CHEESE
NAUGHTIEST DEED: CRAWLING UNDER A FENCE AND CHASING THE BULLS

MIA

WILBUR

PET HATE: BIRDS
FAVOURITE TOY: LEROY
OWNER: ZOE CRITTENDEN
FAVOURITE PASTIME: SLEEPING
OBSESSIONS: TAPE MEASURE,
RAKE, LEAF BLOWER AND BROOM
NAUGHTIEST DEED: CHASING THE CHICKENS
FAVOURITE FOOD: ANYTHING EXCEPT HIS OWN DINNER

LEROY

OWNER: FINN KRIEL
FAVOURITE PASTIME: HANGING OUT
HIS WITH BIG BROTHER WILBUR
OBSESSION: SLEEPING IN CUPBOARDS
PET HATE: HAVING HIS HARNESS PUT ON
NAUGHTIEST DEED: CHEWING THE NOSES
OFF ALL OF THE SOFT TOYS IN THE HOUSE
FAVOURITE FOOD: FREE-RANGE CHICKEN EGGS THAT
DROP ON THE GROUND WHEN BEING COLLECTED

MARGAUX

OBSESSION: SHEEP
OWNER: TOM BARRY
PET HATE: HAVING A BATH
FAVOURITE FOOD: STEAK TARTARE (AKA BEEF MINCE)
FAVOURITE TOY: HER GIANT SCOOBY DOO STUFFED TOY
NAUGHTIEST DEED: LEAVING HER MARKS IN THE BOSS'S OFFICE

PET HATE: BROOMS
OWNER: SAM BARRY
OBSESSION: PLAYING CHASEY
FAVOURITE TOY: SQUEAKY PIG
FAVOURITE FOOD: PUPPY MILK PANNA COTTA
NAUGHTIEST DEED: DOING NUMBER TWO IN THE OFFICE

BEATRICE

PEPPER

PET HATE: THE HOSE
OWNER: CRAIG FENNELL
KNOWN ACCOMPLICE: BAXTER
FAVOURITE PASTIME: CHASING RABBITS
FAVOURITE FOOD: ITALIAN PORK AND FENNEL SAUSAGE
FAVOURITE TOY: ENDLESS SUPPLY OF CHEAP TENNIS BALLS
NAUGHTIEST DEED: CHEWING UP CRAIG'S NEW WORK BOOTS

BOMBE ALASKA

OWNER: BEN PORTET
FAVOURITE TOY: BARREL BUNGS
FAVOURITE FOOD: BOMBE ALASKA
KNOWN ACCOMPLICES: LOUIS AND BOB
PET HATE: GETTING OUT OF HER WARM BED
OBSESSION: HUNTING RABBITS (WITHOUT LUCK)
FAVOURITE PASTIME: CHASING KANGAROOS THROUGH VINEYARDS

MAGGIE

PET HATE: SOCIALISING
FAVOURITE TOY: LEAVES
OBSESSION: CHASING LEAVES
OWNER: NIGEL VAN DER ZANDE
FAVOURITE PASTIME: SITTING UNDER THE UTE
NAUGHTIEST DEED: NOT STAYING WHEN
THE UTE IS OUT AND ABOUT IN THE VINEYARD

KOOP

FAVOURITE TOY: BUNG
OWNER: STEPHEN DEW
KNOWN ACCOMPLICE: WES THE HORSE
FAVOURITE FOOD: SMOKED SALMON PASTA WITH SHAVED TRUFFLE
NAUGHTIEST DEED: DRAGGING A DEAD KANGAROO TO THE BACK DOOR

DAPHNE

OBSESSION: BIRDS
OWNER: REID BOSWARD
FAVOURITE FOOD: CAT FOOD
PET HATE: ACTION OF ANY SORT
FAVOURITE PASTIME: BEING A CAT
NAUGHTIEST DEED: LEAVING WOHLERS WITHOUT PAYING HER BILL

OBSESSION: FOOD
FAVOURITE TOY: BONES
OWNER: SARAH MACMAHON
FAVOURITE PASTIME: EATING
NAUGHTIEST DEED: EATING TRUFFLES
FROM UNDER THE CHRISTMAS TREE
PET HATE: OTHER DOGS EATING HER FOOD

JESS

SONNY

FAVOURITE TOY: DUSTPAN BRUSH
OWNERS: MAL AND EMMA SWARBRICK
NAUGHTIEST DEEDS: THE '2013 MASSACRE' AND
CHASING MANFRED THE MINIATURE HORSE
PET HATES: BEING LEFT BEHIND AND CHICKENS
FAVOURITE PASTIMES: CHASING GUMNUTS AND GOING FOR A DRIVE
OBSESSION: LOOKING FOR SKINKS UNDER THE CELLAR DOOR VERANDAH

FAVOURITE TOY: BARK
FAVOURITE FOOD: CHEESE
OBSESSION: PLAYING WITH BARK
NAUGHTIEST DEED: STEALING A
WHEEL OF BRIE FROM A COFFEE TABLE
OWNER: MARGARET VAN DER MEULEN
FAVOURITE PASTIME: MEETING CELLAR DOOR VISITORS
PET HATE: ANYONE WHO WON'T SAY HELLO AT THE CELLAR DOOR

BETTY

WHISKEY

OWNERS: THE MAY FAMILY

FAVOURITE PASTIME: RIDING ON THE FOUR-WHEEL MOTORBIKE

OBSESSION: STALKING MAGPIES

FAVOURITE FOOD: 'CHUNKERS' CHICKEN WITH SCRAMBLED EGGS AND PARSLEY

NAUGHTIEST DEED: SITTING BETWEEN A BRIDE AND GROOM DURING THEIR WEDDING CEREMONY

PET HATE: THE CHICKENS TRYING TO STEAL HIS FOOD

OWNER: DION TURNER
FAVOURITE TOY: TENNIS BALLS
PET HATE: BEING GROWLED AT (CAUSING
HIM TO HIDE UNDER THE SHED FOR THE DAY)
OBSESSION: WRESTLING WITH HIS MATE BUCKLEY
FAVOURITE FOOD: LAMB RACK SCRAPS FROM THE RESTAURANT
NAUGHTIEST DEED: CHEWING UP BEAN BAGS ON THE FRONT LAWN
FAVOURITE PASTIME: HUNTING WITH HIS MATE FRITZ THE WHIPPET

GUS

PEPPER

OWNER: CASSIE FARR
PET HATE: LOUD NOISES
FAVOURITE TOY: SOCCER BALL
FAVOURITE FOOD: COOKED LAMB HEARTS
FAVOURITE PASTIME: RIDING FRONT SEAT ON THE KUBOTA RV
OBSESSIONS: TILLY (GARY FARR'S DOG) AND GUARDING HER MUM
NAUGHTIEST DEED: CLIMBING UNDER THE BED TO SLEEP AT NIGHT

COOPER

FAVOURITE FOOD: LAMB ROAST
OWNERS: NICK AND CASSIE FARR
FAVOURITE TOY: THE BABY'S SQUEAKY TOYS
FAVOURITE PASTIMES: CHASING SHADOWS AND
BEING INVOLVED IN ALL ASPECTS OF HUMAN LIFE
OBSESSIONS: NAVIGATING THE FORKLIFT AND SCHMACKOS AT BEDTIME
NAUGHTIEST DEEDS: LICKING THE BABY'S HEAD AND STEALING CAT FOOD

OBSESSION: PIZZA
FAVOURITE FOOD: PIZZA
OWNER: ANDREW RYAN
PET HATE: SMALL FLUFFY WHITE DOGS
FAVOURITE TOYS: GRETCHEN'S TEDDYS
FAVOURITE PASTIME: CHASING RABBITS
NAUGHTIEST DEED: DESTROYING CUSTOM-DESIGNED
FASCINATORS THE NIGHT BEFORE THE SPRING CARNIVAL

EVIE

PET HATE: PLOVERS
FAVOURITE FOOD: STEAK
FAVOURITE TOY: MONKEY
OWNER: ADAM CARNABY
OBSESSIONS: RIPPING FLUFFY TOYS
APART AND GENERALLY ANNOYING PEOPLE
NAUGHTIEST DEED: JUMPING INTO A STRANGER'S CAR
FAVOURITE PASTIMES: GOING FOR WALKS AND CHASING RABBITS

LULU

HUGO

FAVOURITE PASTIME: RUNNING
FAVOURITE TOY: DEER ANTLERS
NAUGHTIEST DEED: TEARING PAPER
TO SHREDS IN THE LIVING ROOM
OWNERS: DOROTHY AND NIGEL GALLOP
FAVOURITE FOODS: YOGHURT AND HONEY

PET HATE: CIGAR SMOKE
FAVOURITE FOOD: CHICKEN
FAVOURITE TOY: RUBBER PIG
NAUGHTIEST DEED: CHEWING THE TOE
OUT FROM DOROTHY'S VERSACE SHOES
OWNERS: DOROTHY AND NIGEL GALLOP
FAVOURITE PASTIME: CHASING RABBITS

HENRI

ROXY

OBSESSION: CHEWING
OWNER: KARREN LEWIS
NAUGHTIEST DEED: BUTTING THINGS
FAVOURITE FOODS: ROSES AND CAMELLIAS
FAVOURITE PASTIME: SLEEPING IN FRONT OF THE FIRE

KNOWN ACCOMPLICE: RALPHIE
OBSESSIONS: FOOD AND PLAYING FETCH
PET HATES: RABBITS AND BLUE-TONGUE LIZARDS
OWNERS: OLIVIA, IRENE AND ROBERT MAGDZIARZ
FAVOURITE TOY: ANYTHING SHE CAN PLAY FETCH WITH.
FAVOURITE PASTIMES: EATING AND GOING TO THE BEACH
NAUGHTIEST DEED: TRYING TO GET OUT OF THE YARD TO EAT RABBITS

LAYLA

OBSESSION: BERNARD THE MAGPIE
PET HATE: THE SMELL OF FOXES
WHEN HE GOES OUT AT NIGHT FOR A PEE
OWNERS: ANDREW AND HOLLY MARSH
NAUGHTIEST DEED: JUMPING OFF THE BACK
OF THE UTE AND BREAKING HIS BACK LEG
FAVOURITE PASTIME: MISTAKING CURLY-HAIRED
POPPY MARSH FOR A SHEEP AND CHASING HER AROUND

SPOOK

EVIE

OWNER: BRETT WINSLOW
OBSESSION: GARDENING AT CELLAR DOOR
KNOWN ACCOMPLICES: STELLA AND MARGARET THE CAT
PET HATES: SUDDEN MOVEMENTS AND SMALL CHILDREN
FAVOURITE TOYS: RUBBER RAT AND MARGARET THE CAT
FAVOURITE FOOD: LEFTOVERS FROM FRIDAY AFTERNOON BBQS
NAUGHTIEST DEED: DIGGING UP THE PLANTS AT CELLAR DOOR

FAVOURITE TOY: MISS PIGGY
OWNERS: THE BROWN FAMILY
FAVOURITE FOOD: THE NEXT MEAL
OBSESSION: HUMPING HIS BLANKET
PET HATE: THE THOUGHT OF SLEEPING OUTSIDE
NAUGHTIEST DEED: EATING DYNAMIC LIFTER FROM THE GARDEN
FAVOURITE PASTIME: STEALING ATTENTION FROM HIS OLDER SISTERS

GUS

LABRADOR X · 18 WEEKS · **BROWN BROTHERS** MILAWA, VIC 129

"If your dog doesn't like someone,
you probably shouldn't either."

JOHN WAYNE

a DOG of a WINEMAKER

by Tyson Stelzer

I'VE ALWAYS THOUGHT a dog would make an outstanding chief winemaker.

Picture man's best friend raising a paw to give the green light to commence harvest, barking commands in the tasting room, rising majestically in his place to signal the final decision on the year's blend.

An insane suggestion? No dog can drive a tractor, prune a vine, climb a ladder to assess a ferment, connect a hose, turn on a tap. He can't even lift a glass or pick a bunch of grapes (without eating it).

But what chief winemaker ever busies themselves with such menial tasks? There's always an army of cellarhands, vineyard workers and lab techs on hand, leaving the most important decisions to, well, the top dog. And in this role our canine friend is particularly gifted.

Ask any winemaker to name their most prized asset and they will invariably point to their nose.

Meet Nick Carter. The grandfather of Bloodhound trailing folklore, Nick was born in 1900 and credited with more than 650 finds in his life, including successfully following a trail already an incredible twelve days old.

So extraordinary is the Bloodhound's sense of smell that the breed has gained fame the world over for tracking escaped prisoners, missing people, lost children and lost pets. A Bloodhound has sniffed out termites, drugs, explosives, guns, leaking gas pipes, bedbugs and even cancerous tumours.

Bloodhounds can track scents days later, where no tracks are visible, over great distances, even across water. They have been known to follow a human trail for more than eighty kilometres, locate bodies under water, even grave sites in flood-ravaged areas.

While you and I have some ten million olfactory receptor cells, the average dog is endowed with 200 million and a Bloodhound more than four billion.

In a winery, such superhuman sensitivity could revolutionise the way wine is made.

And it already has. Miss Louisa Belle has an important responsibility at Linnaea Vineyards in Melbourne. The seven-year-old red Bloodhound ensures no cork taint contaminates a single bottle. Cork taint destroys wine, leaving it tasting like damp cardboard or even, funnily enough, wet dog. Not at Linnaea. Faced with a pile of corks, Miss Belle can isolate a tainted cork and push it aside with her snout within thirty seconds. Just a sniff of a barrel of wine will tell her whether it's off.

And, most useful of all, her owners claim she can even identify a tainted wine before the bottle is opened. Now there's a dog every wine drinker could do with!

Miss Belle is not unique. Labradors can learn that trick, too. Ziggy is a five-year-old fox-red Labrador retriever at Sojourn Cellars in Sonoma, California. So sensitive is her nose that she can detect cork taint in concentrations as low as one part per trillion. That's one-twentieth of a drop in an Olympic swimming pool.

I can see it now, packs of Bloodhounds and Labradors scouring Portuguese cork sheds with the military precision of the border protection dogs in a Heathrow arrivals hall. Had it happened years ago, the entire alternative closures industry may well have been barking up the wrong tree. In today's age of screw caps, there may seem little use for even the best cork taint detector, but higher purposes call for the superhuman sensitivity of our canine friends.

Joy is a Golden Retriever who spends her days bounding along every row of Domaine Chandon's Napa Valley vineyards. She's on the hunt for something so tiny it's barely visible to the human eye, with a scent imperceptible to the human nose. Undetected, an outbreak of mealy bugs could destroy the entire crop.

After just eight weeks of training, Joy can successfully sniff out a single mealy bug scent planted in the vineyard by her trainer.

As remarkable as these stories are, there's a lot more to winemaking than simply identifying bad corks and bad vines. Is a dog even capable of recognising a good wine if one is put in front of its superhuman nose?

Louisa Belle can sniff out cork taint a mile off, but her owners admit she has no taste for wine, preferring a bowl of water and a generous helping of dog food. Could a dog even reliably recognise wine?

If any old lab rat can do it, surely our clever Bloodhounds and Labradors have a fighting chance. When Japanese researchers tested thirsty mice trained to discriminate between different liquors, they discovered that they could reliably distinguish red wine from white wine, rosé wine, sake and plum liqueur. But when it came to distinguishing cheap Japanese cask reds from Beaujolais Villages, most mice failed the test.

If a mouse can't pick one red wine from another, can a dog? And, more importantly, can it pick a dreadful one from a good one? Winemaking at its core is built on an aesthetic appreciation, an ability to identify quality fruit, the best batches and the finest blends. Surely a dog can't be trained to do that?

Or can it? The clue this time comes from a place even more unlikely than lab rats. A study that seems to all intents and purposes bird-brained, yet which earned its researchers nothing less than a Nobel

prize. The premise was as simple as it was absurd: could a pigeon be trained to be an art critic?

Birds were trained to peck at a button for good paintings and do nothing in response to bad works. With never-seen works, pigeons picked good paintings twice as often as bad paintings. They successfully discriminated good from bad, watercolours from pastels, even Picasso from Monet.

If a tiny-brained pigeon can appreciate artistic excellence, surely a clever dog is capable of recognising great wine. And if it can recognise it, is there any reason it couldn't be trained to make it?

With the right conditioning, a Bloodhound, Labrador or even a little Beagle could be conditioned to roam the rows of a vineyard, munching on grapes and giving the signal to flag the start of harvest.

He could call the shots at the receival bin, sensitively nosing every batch of incoming grapes, making the decision to declassify or promote. And with the right training, why couldn't he make the call on when to take it out of oak, choose the best of the blending options and select the right time to release it to the market?

Don't be surprised when a dog's name one day appears as the chief winemaker on the back of your favourite bottle, signed with a paw print. It's about time some noble winemaker put the reins into the paws of their canine companion. With the PR they'd generate, the wine would be an instant sellout. Even if it were a dog's breakfast.

TYSON STELZER IS THE INTERNATIONAL WINE & SPIRIT COMMUNICATOR OF THE YEAR 2015, AUSTRALIAN WINE COMMUNICATOR OF THE YEAR 2013 AND INTERNATIONAL CHAMPAGNE WRITER OF THE YEAR 2011. HE IS A TELEVISION PRESENTER, REGULAR CONTRIBUTOR TO 15 MAGAZINES AND AUTHOR OF 15 WINE BOOKS, THOUGH DOESN'T YET CONSIDER HIMSELF AN 'OLD DOG' IN THE WORLD OF WINE WRITING. THIS STORY HAS BEEN REPRINTED FROM *WINE DOGS AUSTRALIA 3*, PUBLISHED 2012.

OWNER: GRAEME SCOTT
FAVOURITE FOOD: BANANA
FAVOURITE PASTIME: DISPLAYING FRENETIC
BURSTS OF ENERGY FOLLOWED BY SLEEP
OBSESSION: COLLECTING AND STORING ITEMS
FOR CHEWING AND PLAYING WITH LATER
NAUGHTIEST DEED: JUMPING ONTO THE TABLE AND PEEING
IN EXCITEMENT (WITH A LITTLE GOING IN THE PORRIDGE)

REX

ISABELLA

FAVOURITE PASTIMES: CHOMPING ON BONES
AND ROLLING IN FRESHLY CUT GRASS
FAVOURITE FOODS: SARDINES AND BACON
OWNERS: BRETT AND KATHRYN WOODWARD
OBSESSIONS: BALL, BALL, BALL, BONE, BALL, BALL, BALL
NAUGHTIEST DEED: POOPING ON THE MEMBERS' ROOM CARPET
PET HATES: PLASTIC GROCERY BAGS AND NEXT DOOR'S YAPPY WHITE DOG

OBSESSION: THE CLOTHES LINE
FAVOURITE TOY: A PIECE OF WINERY HOSE
FAVOURITE PASTIMES: MUSTERING THE CAR
AND RUNNING IN CIRCLES UNDER THE CLOTHES LINE
PET HATES: WATER PISTOLS AND BEING WASHED
OWNERS: KRISTIN, MARISSA AND AMBER McLARTY
NAUGHTIEST DEEDS: BREAKING THE CLOTHES LINE
AND RUNNING OVER TO CELLAR DOOR FOR FUN AND FOOD

PIP

HUGO

OWNER: STEPHEN JUNK
PET HATE: HAVING A BATH
FAVOURITE TOY: PLASTIC BOTTLE
OBSESSIONS: FOOD AND CHASING ANIMALS
NAUGHTIEST DEED: DISAPPEARING IN THE
BUSH FOR HOURS LOOKING FOR KANGAROOS
FAVOURITE PASTIME: HUNTING FOR KANGAROOS

OWNER: OLA TYLESTAM
FAVOURITE TOY: TENNIS BALL
OBSESSION: ANNOYING THE ALPACAS
NAUGHTIEST DEED: ROLLING IN DUCK POO
PET HATE: SHARING A BED WITH THE OTHER DOGS
FAVOURITE PASTIME: CHASING AND RETRIEVING BALLS

XENA

BECKY

FAVOURITE PASTIME: LONG
WALKS WITH A FULL BELLY
FAVOURITE TOY: SCHOOL SOCKS
OBSESSION: COLLECTING ROCKS
OWNERS: THE KERRIGAN FAMILY
FAVOURITE FOOD: CAFÉ DOG TREATS
NAUGHTIEST DEED: DIGGING UP IRRIGATION PIPES

OWNER: RODERICK MICALLEF
PET HATES: MAGPIES AND PATS
OBSESSIONS: ROD AND CHASING ANYTHING
FAVOURITE TOY: SOMETHING FLUFFY THAT HE CAN TEAR APART
NAUGHTIEST DEEDS: RIPPING UP THE COUCH AND SHREDDING TOWELS
FAVOURITE FOODS: ZONZO WOODFIRED PIZZA AND MEDIUM-RARE STEAK
FAVOURITE PASTIMES: SWIMMING IN THE DAM AND RIDING IN THE BACK OF THE UTE

DIESEL

PEANUT

OBSESSION: VISITORS
OWNERS: JANE AND PETER BAILEY
NAUGHTIEST DEED: BITING INTO DUVETS
FAVOURITE FOOD: CHUNKS OF STEAK HE
OCCASIONALLY GETS FOR PILL-HIDING PURPOSES
FAVOURITE PASTIME: TAKING THE LONG ROUTE ON HIS MORNING WALKS

WOODY NOOK WINES WILYABRUP, WA | BOXER X, 9

NAUGHTIEST DEED:
DIGGING TO GET ATTENTION

FAVOURITE PASTIME:
PLAYING WITH SCARLETT BURTON

FAVOURITE FOOD: LAMB SHANK

OBSESSION: BARKING AT SCHOOL
KIDS WALKING PAST THE HOUSE

OWNERS: MATT AND RENEE BURTON

OBSESSION: TALKING

FAVOURITE FOOD:
SCARLETT'S LEFTOVER TOAST

NAUGHTIEST DEED:
SNEAKING INTO THE HOUSE

PET HATE: THUNDERSTORMS

OWNERS: MATT AND RENEE BURTON

FAVOURITE PASTIME: HIS DAILY WALK

FAVOURITE FOOD:
WHATEVER ELLIOTT'S EATING

OBSESSION: BEING OVER-
AFFECTIONATE WITH PEOPLE

FAVOURITE PASTIME: EATING
DINNER AS FAST AS POSSIBLE

PET HATE: GETTING INTO TROUBLE

OWNERS: MATT AND RENEE BURTON

GOLDEN RETRIEVERS, 8, 10 & 6 | **GUNDOG ESTATE** POKOLBIN, NSW

WILLOW

PET HATE: WATER
OBSESSION: BEAR (THE CAT)
OWNERS: ROSEMARY AND TERRY BENNETT
NAUGHTIEST DEED: RUNNING AWAY FROM HER OWNERS
FAVOURITE TOYS: A LARGE TOY SOFT DOG CALLED HAMISH
FAVOURITE FOODS: ARROWROOT BISCUITS AND ICE CREAM
FAVOURITE PASTIME: HURDLING THE BOX HEDGES IN THE GARDEN

HOME HILL WINERY RANELAGH, TAS | WEIMARANER, 2

FAVOURITE TOY: ROCKS
OBSESSION: ROCK DIVING
FAVOURITE PASTIME: FISHING
OWNERS: JULIE AND SEAN BENNETT
NAUGHTIEST DEED: BREAKING HIS TEETH ON ROCKS
PET HATE: NOT BEING ALLOWED TO GO ROCK COLLECTING

BARNEY

BONNIE

FAVOURITE TOY: CIAO
FAVOURITE PASTIMES: EATING
AND WRESTLING WITH CIAO
NAUGHTIEST DEED: DIGGING
HOLES TO CURL UP AND NEST IN
PET HATE: OBJECTS CRAMPING
HER STYLE IN THE BACK OF THE UTE
OWNERS: ANDREW AND KATRINA GAY

OWNER: TONY BRYANT
OBSESSION: CHASING BALLS
FAVOURITE PASTIMES: GREETING
CUSTOMERS AND CHEWING STICKS
FAVOURITE TOYS: BALLS AND STICKS
NAUGHTIEST DEED: INADVERTENTLY
DESTROYING GRANDCHILDREN'S SPORTS BALLS
PET HATE: F-BOMBS EXPLODING AT HIGH VOLUME

CIAO

the WINERY HOUND

by Dave Brookes

THE WINERY HOUND is indeed a wondrous creature. At a time when the pressures of the wine industry can seem overwhelming, it is often the humble winery dog that lifts the spirits and puts a smile on one's face. The menial tasks around the winery are transformed by their companionship. Driving a forklift, be it moving barrels in the shed or loading a truck, seems slightly easier with a smiling, four-legged navigator sitting beside you. Filling an endless line-up of barrels, once you factor out trying to find a bung that isn't distorted by chewing and doesn't have teeth marks all over it, seems a lot less onerous when you have a tail-wagging companion leaping from barrel to barrel to keep you amused.

And of course if you bugger something up and your only witness is the winery dog.... your secret is safe.... In fact it was *Grapes of Wrath* author John Steinbeck who remarked "I've seen a look in dogs' eyes, a quickly vanishing look of amazed contempt, and I am convinced that basically dogs think humans are nuts."

During smoko they are an enthusiastic and indeed, handy repository for any gluten-free abominations that have been surreptitiously stashed in your lunchbox by your well-meaning better half. Come knock off, when you slide your wine-splattered legs into a chair and twist the top off a frothy beverage to celebrate the end of a long day, the winery dog will be at your side, circling the table, checking everyone in turn, ensuring all have the requisite beverage in return for an encouraging scratch behind the ears.

English playwright George Bernard Shaw most poignantly remarked that "If you eliminate smoking and gambling, you will be amazed to find that almost all an Englishman's pleasures can be, and mostly are, shared by his dog," and it is pleasantly reassuring to see that our vinous canine companions seemingly enjoy "knock-off drinks" just as much as their exhausted two-legged brethren and sistren.

They can be a fine welcoming committee for winery and cellar door visitors. Though I do remember one time being alerted by a beeping horn and venturing outside to see a car-load of petrified Chinese visitors whose car was being encircled by four smiling, barking winery hounds, more than happy to see some new faces.

Sinophobia aside, they are for the most part most accommodating when visitors arrive; sometimes lacking the energy to raise themselves from a prone position but you will at the very least get a raise of the eye and a wag of the tail in recognition of your presence.

We tend to worry too much, and time spent with them can erase any niggling doubts or calm one's thoughts. Some hard-charging retailer has slashed the price on one of our wines to $12 a bottle by the case?... pfffttttt... That's $84 in 'dog dollars'... Don't worry about it.

When I started writing this I was going to sit down and write a job description and advertisement for an opening at a winery for a winery dog. And, with great clarity I came to a realisation. There is no job description for the winery hound. They just are and they just have to be there. As Quentin Tarantino says "Dogs got personality. Personality goes a long way."

DAVID BROOKES IS A WINE WRITER/MARKETER, PRESENTER AND WINE JUDGE LIVING IN SOUTH AUSTRALIA'S EDEN VALLEY. HE DIVIDES HIS TIME BETWEEN PLAYING HIS GUITAR ON THE PORCH, STARING UP AT BIG GUM TREES AND TRAVELLING AUSTRALIA AND OVERSEAS RESEARCHING WINE STORIES. HE IS THE PROUD FATHER OF DUDLEY THE WONDER DOG, A CAT, A SHEEP, SEVEN DUCKS AND A COUPLE OF CHOOKS. HE SPENDS TOO MUCH ON WINE.

OBSESSION: WATER
OWNER: FILIPPO BARRECA
FAVOURITE FOOD: SCHMACKOS
FAVOURITE TOY: OLD BLUNDSTONE WORK BOOT
NAUGHTIEST DEED: UPROOTING ENTIRE GARDENS
FAVOURITE PASTIME: SLEEPING IN HER WINE BARREL KENNEL
PET HATE: GETTING TOLD OFF FOR UPROOTING ENTIRE GARDENS

TRIPPA

OWNER: SEB SCHAAD
FAVOURITE TOY: BUNG
PET HATE: THE POSSUMS IN THE ROOF
FAVOURITE PASTIME: LYING IN THE SUN
OBSESSIONS: LICKING AND CONSTANTLY SEARCHING FOR FOOD
NAUGHTIEST DEED: SNATCHING A COUPLE OF OUR FEATHERED FRIENDS

BROKENWOOD WINES POKOLBIN, NSW | ROTTWEILER X 2

OWNER: PHIL LE MESSURIER
FAVOURITE TOY: TENNIS BALL
FAVOURITE FOOD: MEAT AND 3 VEG
PET HATE: TECHNOLOGY BEING TURNED ON
OBSESSION: ANYTHING THAT TAKES FLIGHT
FAVOURITE PASTIME: SWIMMING AT THE BEACH
NAUGHTIEST DEED: TAKING A ROAST CHOOK OFF THE TABLE

MONTY

PET HATE: SEAGULLS AT THE BEACH
OWNERS: ELIZABETH AND TRAVIS WRAY
FAVOURITE FOOD: OTHER PEOPLE'S MUFFINS
FAVOURITE TOY: HIS YELLOW SHERRIN FOOTBALL
OBSESSION: CARRYING HONKEY NUTS IN HIS MOUTH
NAUGHTIEST DEED: EATING GRAPES OUT OF THE PICKING BINS
FAVOURITE PASTIME: GETTING TUMMY RUBS IN THE CELLAR DOOR

OWNER: GWYN OLSEN
PET HATE: BRIDESMAIDS
OBSESSION: CHASING LIZARDS
FAVOURITE FOOD: PEANUT BUTTER ON TOAST
FAVOURITE TOYS: BARREL BUNGS AND FRISBEE
NAUGHTIEST DEED: JUMPING ON THE CFO'S DESK AND EATING
A PIECE OF CAKE HE HAD BEEN SAVING FOR AFTERNOON TEA

SPENCER

POPPY

FAVOURITE PASTIMES: CHASING
GUMNUTS AND GREETING VISITORS
PET HATE: HAVING HER PHOTO TAKEN
OWNERS: BEC AND PETER PHILLICUS
FAVOURITE TOY: ANYTHING THAT SQUEAKS
OBSESSION: CHASING GUMNUTS AND BALLS
FAVOURITE FOODS: HOMEMADE CHICKEN AND RICE

OWNER: RICHARD ANGOVE
FAVOURITE FOODS: CHICKEN AND CELERY
NAUGHTIEST DEED: USING THE DIRTY WASHING
BASKET AS HIS OWN PERSONAL LUCKY DIP
OBSESSION: BEING INVOLVED WITH EVERYTHING
FAVOURITE PASTIME: SWIMMING AND DIGGING AT MASLIN BEACH
FAVOURITE TOY: ANYTHING CHEWABLE TO THE POINT OF DESTRUCTION

CHALKY

FAVOURITE TOY: HER BED
OWNER: LEANNE ROGERS
NAUGHTIEST DEED: CHASING
THE DUCKS TO STEAL THEIR FOOD
PET HATE: HAVING HER HEAD PATTED
FAVOURITE FOOD: PINOT THE CAT'S DINNER
FAVOURITE PASTIME: SAYING HELLO TO GUESTS

SARI

FRED

OWNER: CASEY WHITE
PET HATE: COMING INSIDE
FAVOURITE TOY: HIS LEAD
FAVOURITE PASTIME:
BEING AS LAZY AS POSSIBLE
NAUGHTIEST DEED: COLLECTING
NEIGHBOURS' BELONGINGS
OBSESSION: COLLECTING THINGS

OWNER: CASEY WHITE
FAVOURITE FOOD: BANANAS
OBSESSION: THE VEGIE PATCH
NAUGHTIEST DEED: EATING
THE WHOLE VEGIE PATCH
FAVOURITE PASTIME:
HAVING HER BELLY SCRATCHED
PET HATE: NOT BEING ALLOWED
INSIDE, ESPECIALLY WHEN IT IS COLD

STELLA

MAX

FAVOURITE PASTIME: BEING THE
WORLD'S FASTEST COUCH POTATO
PET HATE: THE SMELL OF HIS OWN GAS
NAUGHTIEST DEEDS: STEALING GUESTS'
PICNICS AND CLEARING THE ROOM WITH GAS
OBSESSION: CATCHING THE VACUUM CLEANER
OWNERS: CRAIG AND JENNIFER BRENT-WHITE
FAVOURITE FOOD: A GOOD BBQ FOLLOWED BY ICE CREAM

MONTY

NAUGHTIEST DEED: HUMPING
FAVOURITE PASTIME: LICKING
SPILT WINE FROM BARREL TOPPING
FAVOURITE FOOD: BLUE SWIMMER
CRABS AND DHUFISH LIGHTLY GRILLED
OWNERS: CRAIG AND JENNIFER BRENT-WHITE
OBSESSION: HUMPING MAX AT EVERY OPPORTUNITY
PET HATE: NOT GETTING HER TEN HOURS BEAUTY SLEEP

OWNER: RAURI DONKIN
PET HATE: HAVING A BATH
OBSESSION: FOOD, FOOD, FOOD
NAUGHTIEST DEED: RIPPING LAUNDRY
OFF THE LINE AND USING IT TO MAKE A BED
FAVOURITE FOODS: CHICKEN NECKS AND MARROWBONE
FAVOURITE PASTIME: GETTING A TUMMY SCRATCH IN THE SUN

SALA

JEEPERS

PET HATE: YOUNG UPSTARTS
FAVOURITE PASTIME: SLEEPING
FAVOURITE FOOD: SOMETHING SOFT
OWNERS: MARK AND VIKKI MESSENGER
NAUGHTIEST DEED: SILENT DEADLY FARTS
FAVOURITE TOY: TOYS ARE FOR YOUNG UPSTARTS
OBSESSION: DREAMING OF CHASING BUNGS FROM BARRELS

PET HATE: CYCLISTS
FAVOURITE TOY: BUNGS
OBSESSION: ANYTHING WITH TYRES
OWNERS: JESS AND JASON CHRCEK
KNOWN ACCOMPLICE: WALLACE FROM ELLIOT ROCKE
FAVOURITE FOODS: BACON AND LUNCH PLATTER LEFTOVERS
NAUGHTIEST DEED: BITING TYRES ON CARS, BIKES AND TROLLEYS

BARNEY

HAMISH

OWNER: NAT BURCH
FAVOURITE FOOD: LONG-LASTING BONES
FAVOURITE TOYS: STUFEED TOYS FROM
THE KIDS' SECTION IN CELLAR DOOR
PET HATES: GRASS SEEDS AND HAIRCUTS
OBSESSIONS: BUGS AND PROTECTING
THE HOUSE AT NIGHT FROM MOVING OBJECTS
FAVOURITE PASTIME: ROLLING OVER FOR CELLAR DOOR VISITORS
NAUGHTIEST DEED: PLAYING MIND GAMES WITH ONCOMING VEHICLES

PET HATE: BATH TIME
FAVOURITE PASTIMES: EATING,
SLEEPING AND CHASING ROOS
FAVOURITE TOY: TED THE TURTLE
OWNERS: MARY AND EUGENE HARMA
NAUGHTIEST DEED: TUCKING INTO THE
GROCERIES WHILE WAITING IN THE CAR
KNOWN ACCOMPLICES: CHEWIE, ALI AND SAKI

DUDLEY

FAVOURITE FOOD: ROO BONES
PET HATE: BRONNIE'S HAIRDRYER
OWNERS: RICK AND BRONNIE BURGE
FAVOURITE TOY: AN AGEING SOFT TOY CALLED DEREK
FAVOURITE PASTIME: CUDDLES WITH BRONNIE ON THE COUCH
OBSESSION: WOWING PEOPLE WITH HIS 'OTTER' IMPERSONATIONS

FAVOURITE FOOD: RABBIT
PET HATE: VACUUM CLEANER
OWNERS: RICK AND BRONNIE BURGE
NAUGHTIEST DEED: STEALING AND EATING
SAUSAGES IN THE CAR GOING HOME
OBSESSION: BEING THE CENTRE OF ATTENTION
FAVOURITE PASTIME: RIDING IN THE TRUCK WITH RICK

DAISY

DIGBY

PET HATE: BEING IGNORED
OBSESSION: ANNOYING COCO
FAVOURITE TOY: SMELLY SOCKS
FAVOURITE FOODS: CHEESE AND CHOCOLATE
OWNERS: CHESTER OSBORN AND KATH TIDEMANN
NAUGHTIEST DEED: STEALING A KILO OF CHEESE FROM THE KITCHEN
FAVOURITE PASTIMES: DESTROYING DOORMATS AND STEALING FOOD

OBSESSIONS: FOOD AND BONES
PET HATES: STORMS AND THE VET
FAVOURITE PASTIME: FOX HUNTING
OWNERS: CHESTER OSBORN AND KATH TIDEMANN
FAVOURITE TOY: A CARE BEAR STOLEN FROM A KID'S BED
FAVOURITE FOODS: ANYTHING HUMANS EAT AND CHOOK POO
NAUGHTIEST DEED: GOING ON A 3-KM JAUNT WITH AUDREY THE CAT

COCO

FLYNN

FAVOURITE TOY: BLUE RUBBER DUCK
PET HATES: FOXES AND HAVING A BATH
OWNERS: INGA LIDUMS AND DAVE NEYLE
NAUGHTIEST DEED: FINISHING OFF DAVE'S
TAKEAWAY FLAT WHITE (CUP AND ALL)
FAVOURITE PASTIMES: PADDLING IN THE
DAM AND RIDING IN THE TRUCK WITH DAVE
OBSESSIONS: BARKING AT THE MOON ON QUIET
NIGHTS AND HAVING HIS TUMMY TICKLED

CELLAR·DOOR

DEXTER

FAVOURITE FOOD: EGGS
FAVOURITE TOY: THE BALL
PET HATE: THUNDERSTORMS
OWNERS: BEC AND SCOTT BARR
FAVOURITE PASTIME: PLAYING FETCH WITH
ANY BALL, STICK OR FRISBEE HE CAN FIND
NAUGHTIEST DEED: PRANCING AROUND IN THE
BACKYARD WITH A NEW POT PLANT IN HIS MOUTH
OBSESSION: CHASING BREAKING WAVES AT THE BEACH

BANDIT

PET HATE: THE SCARECROW
OWNERS: BEC AND SCOTT BARR
FAVOURITE PASTIME: FOLLOWING BEC AND
SCOTT AROUND LIKE A LITTLE WHITE SHADOW
FAVOURITE TOY: KEVIN, THE STUFFED KANGAROO
OBSESSION: GETTING ATTENTION FROM DEXTER
NAUGHTIEST DEED: STEALING TOILET ROLLS
AND UNROLLING THEM AROUND THE BACKYARD

PIPPA

OBSESSION: GETTING INSIDE
FAVOURITE TOY: SQUEAKY TOY
OWNER: JEROME SCARBOROUGH
PET HATE: THE CONE OF SHAME FROM THE VET
NAUGHTIEST DEED: DIGGING INTO THE CHOOK PEN
FAVOURITE FOOD: ANYTHING INCLUDING DEAD ROOS
FAVOURITE PASTIMES: PINCHING SOCKS AND TOUCHING UP THE CHOOKS

KAISER: I'M A ROTTWEILER

by Jeni Port

"**AS I WAS SAYING,** just this morning, to Oscar, the bossy bitzer down the road who thinks he owns the footpath: "I'M A ROTTWEILER. DON'T MESS WITH ME."

He thought I was kidding. I set him straight.

I find I often have to resort to physical intimidation to get my message across, but I'm built for it. Not that I'm fat, mind you, just solid.

My doctor likes to keep an eye on these things but as I keep telling him, "Doc, you're wasting your time. I'm solid, as solid as a Rottweiler should be."

Now, my mate Henry, the Newfoundland, he's a real handful of bulging baby fat and fur. He might have to watch that. Just saying.

Do I have anger issues?

I don't think so. I like to be treated as well as the next dog but when someone invades my personal space I let 'em have it. Like the old lady who came up to me when I was at my favourite coffee place in the city, Café Duomo, and stuck her face right into mine. Really, how rude and I told her so.

She took it well. Mum and Dad didn't. I wonder when I will be going back there again 'cause I love Duomo's little Portuguese custard tarts. So tasty.

Excuse me for just a minute, will you...

"Hey you! What do you think you're doing there? Yeah, you the delivery guy on the front step! Get outta here! Go on! Raus!"

My home is my domain. If you are an intruder, especially one of those pesky wine delivery guys, you will get short shrift. Just drop off the wine and run.

What Mum does with all that wine, I don't know, all I do know is I like the toys that come with the wine parcels, especially the ones that jump into the air with a pop! Good fun.

But I never touch the stuff myself.

If I have an indulgence, I think I would say it is toilet rolls, full or empty I don't mind. I love the way they go around and around, rolling and rolling. Mesmerising.

Playing with my little chicken pal, Chico, is also one of the most enjoyable ways to kill a few hours. He's damn good fun to have around, he makes the funniest noises and I just have to join in.

My singing voice – I'm told that I am a very fine baritone – is pretty impressive, even if I do say so.

I can hold a note all right, don't you worry about that, and what's more, not a lesson! I'm a natural.

My Mum calls me her little Pavarotti.

What's a rotti to do?

An encore... of course.

Excuse me for just a minute will you...

"Hey you! Yeah, you, the funny-looking guy with the bulging eyes and shaking hands... "

JENI PORT IS A FREELANCE WINE WRITER BASED IN MELBOURNE, WRITING FOR *THE AGE*, *GOURMET TRAVELLER WINE* MAGAZINE, *WINESTATE* MAGAZINE AND OTHERS. SHE JUDGES WINE THROUGHOUT AUSTRALIA AND IS AN AUTHOR. IN 2014 SHE WAS NAMED WINE COMMUNICATOR OF THE YEAR BY WINE COMMUNICATORS OF AUSTRALIA, A NATIONAL GROUP OF WINE PROFESSIONALS.

SNOWY

OBSESSION: FOOD
FAVOURITE TOY: HIS BED
OWNER: DOMINIC HOWE
FAVOURITE FOOD: THE FOOD KIND
PET HATE: NOT GETTING ENOUGH FOOD
FAVOURITE PASTIMES: RIDING IN THE UTE AND
EATING (PREFERABLY AT THE SAME TIME)
NAUGHTIEST DEED: DRAGGING DEAD KANGAROOS UNDER THE HOUSE

OWNER: DAVID BICKNELL
KNOWN ALIAS: 'LARRY-BOY'
PET HATES: THUNDER AND FIREWORKS
FAVOURITE PASTIMES: GOING TO WORK
AND LETTING OFF UNDER DAVID'S DESK
OBSESSION: BEGGING FOR FOOD IN THE RESTAURANT
NAUGHTIEST DEEDS: EATING ALL OF ANGUS' SIX CHICKENS
AND LEAVING DEPOSITS IN THE MIDDLE OF THE WINERY

LARRY

PINOT

OWNER: TIM LOVETT
PET HATE: THE HOSE
OBSESSION: CHASING EMUS
FAVOURITE TOY: TWO-YEAR-OLD SIA
FAVOURITE FOODS: CHICKEN AND RICE
NAUGHTIEST DEED: DIGGING UP THE VEGIE PATCH
FAVOURITE PASTIME: SLEEPING IN THE FRONT SEAT OF THE CAR

PET HATE: PLASTIC BAGS
FAVOURITE TOY: FRISBEE
OWNER: PHIL HUTCHISON
FAVOURITE FOOD: HUMAN FOOD
OBSESSION: CHASING THE FRISBEE
FAVOURITE PASTIMES: SLEEPING AND EATING
NAUGHTIEST DEED: DESTROYING A WHOLE LOUNGE

OWNER: PAUL ATWOOD
PET HATE: THE LAWNMOWER
FAVOURITE TOY: MR JUMBO BALL
FAVOURITE FOODS: CHICKEN AND RICE
NAUGHTIEST DEED: PULLING STUFFING OUT OF PILLOWS
OBSESSION: RUNNING UP BEHIND YOU AND HITTING YOU WITH A STICK

BUDDY

WILBUR

FAVOURITE TOYS: TENNIS BALLS AND STONES
FAVOURITE PASTIMES: PLAYING BALL WITH
THE FORKLIFT AND BEING SITE SUPERVISOR
NAUGHTIEST DEED: PRESSING AUTO-LOCK
WHILE INSIDE THE CAR (WITH THE KEYS)
FAVOURITE FOOD: SIX-DAY-OLD RABBIT
OWNERS: SIMON AND KENDY COWHAM

LUCY

OBSESSION: SOCKS
PET HATE: THUNDER
OWNER: DANIEL DUJIC
FAVOURITE FOOD: MUFFINS
FAVOURITE TOY: BARREL BUNG
NAUGHTIEST DEED: ROLLING IN DEAD FISH
FAVOURITE PASTIME: STARING AT PEOPLE WHILE THEY'RE EATING

GRACE

OBSESSION: BIRDS
OWNER: DANIEL DUJIC
FAVOURITE FOOD: YOGHURT
PET HATE: HOT AIR BALLOONS
FAVOURITE TOY: STUFFED DUCK
NAUGHTIEST DEED: TOO ANXIOUS TO BE NAUGHTY
FAVOURITE PASTIME: HUNTING MICE AND RABBITS

BETTY

PET HATE: BATH TIME
OWNER: EDWARD TOMLINSON
FAVOURITE PASTIME: DISAPPEARING
NAUGHTIEST DEED: ROLLING IN DEAD FAUNA
FAVOURITE FOODS: CHEESE, CREAM AND FRESH FISH

OWNERS: JOE AND SUE EVANS
NAUGHTIEST DEED: STEALING EASTER EGGS
FAVOURITE FOOD: ANYTHING A HUMAN IS EATING
PET HATES: HOT AIR BALLOONS, BICYCLES AND LETTUCE
FAVOURITE PASTIME: SITTING IN HIS WADING POOL IN SUMMER
FAVOURITE TOY: BALLS (CAN THROW THEM FOR HIMSELF IF REQUIRED)

RUA

OBSESSION: SHOES
FAVOURITE TOY: SHOES
FAVOURITE PASTIME: CHASING WHISKERS
OWNERS: DARREN HAUNOLD AND FAMILY
NAUGHTIEST DEED: EATING THE VINEYARD HANDS'
LUNCHES WHILE THEY ARE PICKING AND PRUNING
KNOWN ACCOMPLICES: JASPER AND WHISKERS

BOB

OWNER: CLITIE MURDOCH
FAVOURITE TOY: MUCH-LOVED SQUEAKY BANANA
FAVOURITE PASTIMES: LOOKING CUTE AND
RINGING THE BELLS ON THE DOOR TO BE LET OUTSIDE
NAUGHTIEST DEED: JUMPING INTO CUSTOMERS' CARS
PET HATES: BIKE RIDERS AND PEOPLE WEARING HATS
OBSESSIONS: BROOMS, THE VACUUM CLEANER AND THE WINE TROLLEY

WALLIS

"Dogs and philosophers
do the greatest good
and get the fewest rewards."

DIOGENES LAERTIUS

LIFE in the DOGHOUSE

by Nick Ryan

I'M A MAN WHO SLEEPS SOUNDLY at night secure in the knowledge that if the house were to burn down my better half would only come back to check on me once the dog was safe.

A man needs to know his place. In my case that's a long way behind a Border Collie called Winston.

To be fair, he was hers before she was mine. I brought a precocious daughter to the relationship and she brought a dog named after her favourite champagne.

I'm actually very grateful she's such a Pol Roger fan. I reckon shouting 'Comtes' at the dog park could easily be misheard and lead to some pretty awkward confrontations.

Winston is a product of the 2010 vintage and like the best wines of that fortune-blessed year, he has an elegance and poise that sets him apart from the pack.

He was born a short, slobbering drive from the summer-soaked vineyards of the Hunter Valley but saved at a young age from those strange Northern ways by a Clare Valley girl who let him stretch his puppy legs down long rows of riesling.

She loved him before she loved me so their love is longer. It's not unreasonable to suspect it's deeper too.

The thing is, I can't really blame her. He's better looking than me and even when he's spent the day chasing kangaroos and swimming in the vineyard dam, he's better groomed. Assuming it's his own crap he has been rolling around in and not that of other mutts, he smells better too.

We both have a tendency to throw up when we've exercised too much but he eats his and doesn't just leave it for someone else to clean up. At least he has the decency to look embarrassed when he farts.

Every morning she tells one of us how handsome they are, then yells at the other for forgetting to put the bins out.

The last time she found him with his head in the toilet she went and topped up his water bowl, but when I did it she yelled "That's the last time you go drinking with Andrew Thomas," and stormed off to bed.

And how come his ball obsession is okay just because 'that's what Border Collies do' but as soon as my hand slips inside the waistband of my trackie dacks while I lie on the couch, I'm instantly branded a 'disgusting slob'.

It's not like I haven't tried to assert my authority. I play to my natural strengths as best I can. I exploit the fact that, unlike the dog, I have the ability to enter a restaurant without having to drag a blind person along and I try and seduce her with great food and even better booze.

Things will be going swimmingly, I'll order a bottle of Barolo because she really digs Barolo, and I might start, tentatively at first, to feel that warm inner glow of a man who might just be getting lucky later in the evening. And then somehow, even tucked up in a palatial doghouse at home, Winston comes bounding into our night out.

A sudden storm might break and we'll have to go straight home because Winnie hates thunder. Or a nagging doubt about whether the gate's been closed or not will gnaw at the back of her mind like a starving rat and I'll sit helplessly by as half the deliciousness on her plate ends up in a doggie bag that never fails to deliver on the human-denying threat inherent in its name.

Yet despite all that, I wouldn't change a thing.

Because I reckon this is the best dog I've ever known and he and she are a package deal that I wouldn't give up for a lifetime of magnums of the champagne that inspired his name ... but Jeroboams might be a different matter.

THROWN OUT OF UNIVERSITY IN ADELAIDE AND MOVING TO SYDNEY, **NICK RYAN** USED THE KNOWLEDGE HE'D GAINED RAIDING HIS OLD MAN'S CELLAR TO LAND A JOB WITH ONE OF SYDNEY'S LEADING WINE MERCHANTS. REALISING THAT WRITING ABOUT IT WAS EASIER THAN LIFTING IT HAS LED HIM TO BE A REGULAR CONTRIBUTOR TO *MEN'S STYLE AUSTRALIA, GOURMET TRAVELLER WINE, JAMES HALLIDAY'S WINE COMPANION MAGAZINE* AND ADELAIDE'S *SUNDAY MAIL*. HE IS PASSIONATE ABOUT WINES THAT ARE JUST AS INTERESTING BY THE FOURTH GLASS AS THEY ARE AT THE FIRST AND WOULD GIVE IT ALL UP TO PLAY ONE GAME FOR THE PORT ADELAIDE FOOTBALL CLUB.

MISCHA

OWNERS: THE MYLES FAMILY
FAVOURITE FOOD: ROAST CHICKEN
PET HATE: NOT SLEEPING ON THE BED
FAVOURITE TOYS: RASCAL AND CHARLIE THE CATS
OBSESSION: PLAY FIGHTING WITH RASCAL AND CHARLIE
NAUGHTIEST DEED: EATING HER BABYSITTER'S CURTAINS - TWICE
FAVOURITE PASTIME: COLLECTING THE NEWSPAPER AND MAIL IN THE MORNING

HUMPHREY

FAVOURITE FOOD: METTWURST
OWNERS: DAVID AND NICKI LEHMANN
FAVOURITE PASTIMES: RACING CARS ALONG
THE DRIVEWAY AND HATING THE CAT
NAUGHTIEST DEED: WORKING WITH STELLA
TO SMASH INTO THE GUINEA PIG CAGE
PET HATES: THE VACUUM CLEANER AND THE CAT
FAVOURITE TOY: HIS FLUFFY STUFFED KANGAROO

FAVOURITE TOY: A FRESH APPLE
OWNERS: DAVID AND NICKI LEHMANN
OBSESSION: PICKING AND EATING APPLES
FROM THE APPLE TREE (ONE A DAY)
PET HATE: HUMPHREY HOGGING THE DOG BED
BEFORE SHE HAS A CHANCE TO GET IN FIRST
NAUGHTIEST DEED: THE 'GUINEA PIG' INCIDENT
FAVOURITE PASTIMES: BARKING AT THE CAT AND PICKING APPLES

STELLA

MAX

OWNERS: MARK AND MANDY CREED
FAVOURITE PASTIME: BARKING AT THUNDER
(THINKS IT'S BIG POSSUMS IN TREES)
NAUGHTIEST DEED: BARKING AT ANYONE
WHO DOESN'T THROW A TOY FAST ENOUGH
OBSESSION: DISMEMBERING FLUFFY TOYS
FAVOURITE TOYS: PINE CONES, STICKS AND BALLS
PET HATES: JOGGERS, PUSHBIKES AND DOOR KNOCKING

MERLOT

OWNERS: MARK AND MANDY CREED
FAVOURITE FOOD: WEDDING LEFTOVERS
PET HATES: POSSUMS AND MISSING OUT ON FOOD
OBSESSIONS: STAFF LUNCH AND LEANING ON PEOPLE
FAVOURITE PASTIMES: POKING HIS TONGUE OUT AND
SPENDING RESTAURANT HAPPY HOUR WITH THE GUESTS
NAUGHTIEST DEED: SLEEPING IN THE MOTEL ROOMS WITH GUESTS

OLIVE

OWNER: LEWIS MAXWELL
FAVOURITE FOOD: RABBITS
PET HATE: RABBITS ON THE
WRONG SIDE OF THE FENCE
FAVOURITE PASTIME: HUNTING
OBSESSION: CHASING RABBITS

OWNER: JEREMY MAXWELL
OBSESSION: BUNG CRICKET
FAVOURITE PASTIME: TENNIS
FAVOURITE FOODS: RABBIT AND PAL
FAVOURITE TOYS: ROCKS AND TENNIS BALLS

SOPHIE

POLLY

OWNERS: NEIL AND CATHY HOWARD
FAVOURITE PASTIMES: HUNTING RABBITS
AND GREETING PEOPLE AT CELLAR DOOR
NAUGHTIEST DEED: KILLING TWO CHOOKS
KNOWN ACCOMPLICE: SPIT, THE PET SHEEP
FAVOURITE FOODS: MINCE, BONES AND RABBIT
PET HATE: BEING TIED UP WHEN VISITORS ARRIVE

AXE

OBSESSION: NOISES IN THE NIGHT
FAVOURITE TOY: STUFFED CUSHIONS
OWNERS: CHARLIE AND VIRGINIA MELTON
NAUGHTIEST DEED: EATING A PET MAGPIE
FAVOURITE FOODS: RABBIT AND PET MAGPIES
PET HATE: NOT GETTING FED UNDER THE TABLE
FAVOURITE PASTIME: BARKING AT NOISES AT NIGHT

PET HATE: CLOSED DOORS
OBSESSION: GETTING ATTENTION
FAVOURITE TOY: CAR HEADRESTS
NAUGHTIEST DEED: BEING SECOND
CHEF IN THE PET MAGPIE INCIDENT
FAVOURITE FOOD: AIR-DRIED ROADKILL
OWNERS: CHARLIE AND VIRGINIA MELTON
FAVOURITE PASTIME: ATTENTION-SEEKING

MAJOR

PIPER

PET HATES: CATS AND BATHS

FAVOURITE PASTIMES: DROOLING, EATING AND SNOOZING ON THE COUCH

OBSESSION: STEALING AND RIPPING UP RUBBISH FROM THE BINS NEXT DOOR

NAUGHTIEST DEED: BREAKING HER CERAMIC WATER BOWL THEN EATING SOME OF IT

OWNERS: NADIA, TRISTAN AND DALLAS LUCK

TONIC

OWNER: LINDA POPP

FAVOURITE FOOD: CAT FOOD

FAVOURITE PASTIME: HAVING LUNCH WITH THE CELLAR DOOR STAFF

OBSESSIONS: LINDA AND DRIVING WITH HIS HEAD OUT OF THE CAR WINDOW

NAUGHTIEST DEED: BRINGING LIVE MICE INTO CELLAR DOOR AS GIFTS FOR GUESTS

PET HATES: THUNDER AND BEING LEFT AT HOME

RANGER

PET HATE: THE RUBBISH TRUCK
FAVOURITE FOOD: ANYTHING STOLEN FROM CHEF
OWNERS: SHARON PEARSON AND GARRY SWEENEY
FAVOURITE TOYS: SQUEAKY SNAKE AND SILVER TEA POT
OBSESSIONS: ROLLING IN KANGAROO POO AND STEALING SHINY THINGS
NAUGHTIEST DEED: HIDING ELEVEN SPRINGS FROM THE COUCH IN HIS BED
FAVOURITE PASTIMES: SWIMMING AND JUMPING UP ON BARRELS FOR PATS

What part of 'WOOF' don't you understand?

by Craig McGill and Susan Elliott

JUST ABOUT EVERY WINE GUIDE has a glossary of terminology to help educate people about the fine art of winemaking. Our Wine Dogs books are no exception so, in case some of our readers have come across terms or references that they have found confusing, we hope the following will help them to further understand the wonderful world of oenological canines.

Aroma – the smell of a dog, also referred to as the 'nose' or 'bouquet' of the dog. Hence the term 'that dog is on the nose'.

Balance – a well-balanced Wine Dog is an extraordinary dog of profound and complex character displaying all the attributes expected of a classic canine of its breed. Hounds of this calibre are worth a special effort to find, bring home and love.

Barrique – the French word for a bloody big dog.

Biodognamic – a method of organic dog breeding originally developed by Rudolf Steinwoof. It employs what is described as "a holistic understanding of a dog's life", emphasising spiritual and mystical perspectives. It also references howling at the moon.

Body – the impression of weight or fullness of the dog. The bigger the impression, the more likely a dog is to be referred to as 'full-bodied' such as an Australian cattle dog from the McLaren Vale, as opposed to a 'light-bodied' dog which may be something like a chihuahua from Mudgee.

Botrytis *or* '*Sticky*' – usually a hidden parcel left in the vineyard, (see *Fermentation*). Can contaminate other parts of the winery if left on your shoe.

Brix – a measurement of the intelligence in dogs. The level of brix indicates the degree of the stupidity in the dog. Hence the term 'Thick as a Brix'.

Chook – a chicken.

Clone – dogs originating from a single, individual breed chosen for its specific attributes i.e. clonal selection. Clones can be chosen for companionship, ventriloquism, hunting skills, hard work, slipper retrieval or even juggling.

Corked – a dog that has been spoiled by over-processed dog food, caused by a chemical called *terriblecannedaboli*, or TCA. TCA is also found in the 'bark' of the cork oak tree and is virtually impossible to eradicate.

Dish-licker – Australian term for dog.

DOCG – dog misspelt.

Dog's breakfast – usually a term to describe a winemaker's schedule, journal or diary.

Dry – a dog with a wicked sense of humour and who can deliver a joke with a straight face.

Fermentation – the process of converting a dog's dinner into tomorrow's hidden parcel (see *Botrytis* or '*Sticky*') with the by-product of sulphur dioxide.

Food-friendly – a term to describe a dog, usually a Labrador, that will eat anything and everything.

Hair of the dog – a much-needed alcoholic beverage to help cure a hangover.

Late bloomer – a dog that matures later than average and therefore doesn't reach its full potential until later in life.

Length – how long the dog is.

Meritage – a USA hotel chain for dogs or a mongrel of blended breeds.

Mouth-feel – describes the amount of tennis balls a dog can fit in the mouth such as furry, rubbery, weighty, etc.

Oenodogology – the science and study of Wine Dogs.

Oxidised – a profoundly smelly dog.

Palate – how your leg tastes and feels in a dog's mouth.

Pedigree – a dog with pure breeding, usually with papers and a gold-medal winner.

Plonk – cheap grog and also the title of Australia's best wine documentary.

Punt – the indentation found on the top of a Staffordshire Terrier's head.

Quaffing – the term to describe a Beagle eating dinner.

Reserve – a term widely used to suggest a dog of more superior quality; however, there is no regulation over its use, so it may refer to a Margaret River mongrel or a Hunter Valley pedigree Poodle.

Robust – a dog with a disproportional body/mass index.

Single vineyard – a Wine Dog that has lived only on one particular vineyard.

SO² – Sulphur Dioxide is a pungent and silently excreted gas (usually in the winemaker's office or vehicle).

Super Tuscans – Italian greyhounds, Maremma Sheepdogs and Spinone Italiano.

Terroir – a French term often adopted in other winemaking countries, referring to the environment in which a Wine Dog marks its own territory. A great wine dog is said to reflect its 'terroir' or sense of place usually by rolling in dead things.

Triage – where the vineyard workers eat lunch usually using a special 'triage table' which also provides shade for a sleeping Wine Dog. The dog barely needs to lift it's head to eat any spilled lunch or leftovers.

Varietal – a specific breed.

Vintage – the year the dog was born.

Waiter's Friend – is also a dog.

Wet Dog – a term used for a dog that has just had a bath or a swim in the dam.

Wine Cave – like a man cave but for dogs.

Wine Dogs – *n. Canis vinum* **1**. affable and loyal canines found hanging around the cellar or vineyard. **2**. *[est. 2003]* award-winning series of books celebrating the dogs that live and work in the vineyards, wineries and tasting rooms around the globe. **3**. best friends to the winemakers and the real palate-power behind every successful vintage. **4**. *n.* (slang) *Homo sapien imbibere*; hominid booze hounds who love a good drop. **5**. created all for the love of dogs & wine – www.winedogs.com

PHOTOGRAPHY

Craig with Tule Bollibakka from Silver Oak Cellars, Oakville CA USA

PHOTOGRAPHY © CRAIG MCGILL 2015

SUSAN ELLIOTT

PUBLISHER, DESIGNER

Susan is a multi-skilled artist with a background in fine art, illustration and printmaking. After completing two years of a psychology degree, Sue changed to a career in art. She graduated from The City Art Institute in 1986, majoring in drawing, printmaking and painting.

After two years living abroad, Sue returned to Australia and exhibited her graphic art and screenprints extensively around Sydney, while also working in a number of small design studios. She has developed into an award-winning graphic designer with over 20 years of experience in the industry.

Sue joined McGill Design Group in 1999 as co-owner and Creative Director. She is also co-founder and principal of the Giant Dog publishing house, which is responsible for producing a number of best-selling books, including the *Wine Dogs* titles. She recently designed five *Wine Dogs* stamps for Australia Post.

Sue's knowledge of dogs is unparalleled, and in the past she has also found time to be a successful Siberian Husky breeder. Although currently dogless, Sue loves to spend time with the many wine dogs she meets from around the world as well as a pair of feisty cichlids named Ron and Colin.

CRAIG McGILL

PUBLISHER, PHOTOGRAPHER

Originally from Shepparton in Victoria, Australia, Craig is a self-taught designer and illustrator who started his own design business in Melbourne at 18 years of age. During that time he was appointed as a design consultant to The Reserve Bank of Australia.

His designs and illustrations have graced banknotes throughout the world, including the Australian bicentenary ten-dollar note. His work appears on the original Australian $100 note, Papua New Guinea Kina, Cook Islands Dollars and English Pound traveller's cheques. Craig was also involved in the design and illustration of many countries' security documents such as Passports, Bonds and Traveller's Cheques.

At the age of 23 he designed the entire series of the Cook Islands banknotes and it is believed that he was the world's youngest designer to design a country's

complete currency. In 1991, Craig moved to Sydney where his illustrations were regularly commissioned by agencies and designers both in Australia and around the world.

He is now widely known as Australia's only freelance currency designer. Craig has also designed and illustrated nine stamps for Australia Post. Five of his *Wine Dogs* photos have also been used on stamps for Australia Post.

Craig has been Creative Director of his own agency, McGill Design Group, for over twenty-five years.

Having grown up with a succession of beagles and huskies, Craig is currently road-testing several hundred dog breeds from wineries around the world. www.realnasty.com.au

GIANT DOG PUBLISHING

Giant Dog is a niche independent publishing house specialising in producing benchmark quality design and art books. Recent publications include *Wine Cats*, *Wine Dogs California*, *Wine Dogs Australia 4*, *Wine Dogs Italy*, *Wine Dogs New Zealand 2* and *Footy Dogs*. www.giantdog.com.au

McGILL DESIGN GROUP

McGill Design Group was formed in 1981 and specialises in providing a wide range of quality graphic design services. The studio has produced numerous fine wine labels and packaging as well as corporate identities, advertising, publications and television commercials. www.mcgilldesigngroup.com

WINERY and VINEYARD LISTINGS

NEW SOUTH WALES

Bimbadgen Estate PAGE 157
790 McDonalds Road,
Pokolbin NSW 2320
Ph: (02) 4998 4600
www.bimbadgen.com.au

Briar Ridge Vineyard PAGE 151
593 Mount View Road,
Mount View NSW 2325
Ph: (02) 4990 3670
www.briarridge.com.au

Brokenwood Wines
PAGES 147, 148, 149
McDonalds Road,
Pokolbin NSW 2320
Ph: (02) 4998 7559
www.brokenwood.com.au

**Burnbrae Winery
and Vineyard** PAGE 144
548 Hill End Road,
Mudgee NSW 2850
Ph: (02) 6373 3504
www.burnbraewines.com.au

Elliot Rocke Estate PAGE 177
157 Craigmoor Road,
Mudgee NSW 2850
Ph: (02) 6372 7722
www.elliotrockeestate.com.au

Gundog Estate PAGE 141
101 McDonalds Road,
Pokolbin NSW 2320
Ph: (02) 4998 6873
www.gundogestate.com.au

Hungerford Hill Wines PAGE 28
2450 Broke Road,
Pokolbin NSW 2320
Ph: (02) 4998 7666
www.hungerfordhill.com.au

Huntington Estate PAGE 55
641 Ulan Road,
Mudgee NSW 2850
Ph: (02) 6373 3825
www.huntingtonestate.com.au

James Estate PAGE 133
951 Bylong Valley Way,
Baerami NSW 2333
Ph: (02) 6547 5168

1210 Hermitage Road,
Pokolbin NSW 2320
Ph: (02) 4998 7992
www.jamesestatewines.com.au

Kelman Vineyard PAGE 98
2 Oakey Creek Road,
Pokolbin NSW 2320
Ph: (02) 4991 5456
www.kelmanvineyard.com.au

Lowe Wines PAGES 124, 125
327 Tinja Lane,
Mudgee NSW 2850
Ph: (02) 6372 0800
www.lowewine.com.au

Marsh Estate PAGE 127
Deasys Road,
Pokolbin NSW 2320
Ph: (02) 4998 7587
www.marshestate.com.au

Misty Glen Wines PAGE 107
293 Deasys Road,
Pokolbin NSW 2320
Ph: (02) 4998 7781
www.mistyglen.com.au

Moothi Estate PAGE 159
85 Rocky Waterhole Road,
Mudgee NSW 2850
Ph: (02) 6372 2925
www.moothiestate.com.au

Mount Pleasant Wines PAGE 103
401 Marrowbone Road,
Pokolbin NSW 2320
Ph: (02) 4998 7505
www.mountpleasantwines.com.au

Mudgee Wines Estate PAGE 61
280 Henry Lawson Drive,
Mudgee NSW 2850
Ph: (02) 6372 2244
www.mudgeewines.com.au

Pepper Tree Wines PAGE 21
86 Halls Road,
Pokolbin NSW 2320
Ph: (02) 4909 7100
www.peppertreewines.com.au

Saddler's Creek Wines PAGE 134
15 Marrowbone Road,
Pokolbin NSW 2320
Ph: (02) 4991 1770
www.saddlerscreek.com

**Scarborough Wine
Company** PAGE 166
179 Gillards Road,
Pokolbin NSW 2320
Ph: (02) 4998 7563
www.scarboroughwine.com.au

Shaw Vineyard Estate PAGE 60
34 Isabel Drive,
Murrumbateman NSW 2582
Ph: (02) 6227 5827
www.shawvineyards.com.au

Stargazer PAGE 22
1616 Broke Road,
Pokolbin NSW 2320
Ph: 0408 173 335
www.stargazerwine.com.au

SOUTH AUSTRALIA

Andrew Seppelt Wines PAGE 79
28 Hawke Street,
Kapunda SA 5373
Ph: 0417 883 089
www.andrewseppelt.com

**Angove Family
Winemakers** PAGE 153
117 Chalk Hill Road,
McLaren Vale SA 5171
Ph: (08) 8323 6900
www.angove.com.au

Artwine PAGE 92
72 Bird-in-Hand Road,
Woodside SA 5244
Ph: (08) 8389 9399
www.artwine.com.au

**Ballycroft Vineyard
and Cellars** PAGE 175
1 Adelaide Road,
Greenock SA 5360
Ph: 0488 638 488
www.ballycroft.com

Barossa Chateau PAGE 182
35 Hermann Thumm Drive,
Lyndoch SA 5351
Ph: (08) 8524 4920
www.barossachateau.com

Bremerton Wines PAGE 29
Strathalbyn Road,
Langhorne Creek SA 5255
Ph: (08) 8537 3093
www.bremerton.com.au

Burge Family Winemakers PAGE 162
1312 Barossa Valley Way,
Lyndoch SA
Ph: (08) 8524 4644
www.burgefamily.com.au

Charles Melton Wines PAGE 185
Krondorf Road, Krondorf SA 5352
Ph: (08) 8563 3606
www.charlesmeltonwines.com.au

d'Arenberg PAGE 163
Osborn Road,
McLaren Vale SA 5171
Ph: (08) 8329 4888
www.darenberg.com.au

David Franz Vigneron and Winemaker PAGE 181
94 Stelzer Road, Tanunda SA 5352
Ph: 0419 807 468
www.david-franz.com

DogRidge Vineyards PAGE 13
129 Bagshaws Road,
McLaren Vale SA 5171
Ph: (08) 8383 0140
www.dogridge.com.au

Edenmae Estate Wines PAGE 40
266 Parkers Road,
Mount Pleasant SA 5235
Ph: (08) 8568 2098
www.edenmae.com.au

Fernfield Wines PAGE 165
112 Rushlea Road,
Eden Valley SA 5235
Ph: 0402 788 526
www.fernfieldwines.com.au

Fox Creek Wines PAGE 135
90 Malpas Road,
McLaren Vale SA 5171
Ph: (08) 8557 0000
www.foxcreekwines.com

Golding Wines PAGE 14
52 Western Branch Road,
Lobethal SA 5241
Ph: (08) 8389 5120
www.goldingwines.com.au

Gomersal Wines PAGES 62, 63
203 Lyndoch Road,
Gomersal SA 5352
Ph: (08) 8563 3611
www.gomersalwines.com.au

Good Catholic Girl PAGE 108
20 Main North Road,
Auburn, Clare Valley SA 5451
Ph: 0448 079 406
www.goodcatholicgirl.com.au

Graham Stevens Wines PAGE 24
72 Ingoldby Road,
McLaren Flat SA 5171
Ph: (08) 8383 0997
www.grahamstevenswines.com.au

Greg Cooley Wines PAGE 25
Lot 1, Main North Road,
Clare SA 5453
Ph: (08) 8843 4284
www.gregcooleywines.com.au

Hahndorf Hill Winery PAGES 64, 65
38 Pains Road, Hahndorf SA 5245
Ph: (08) 8388 7512
www.hahndorfhillwinery.com.au

Hardys Tintara PAGE 95
202 Main Road,
McLaren Vale SA 5171
Ph: (08) 8329 4110
www.accolade-wines.com.au

Henschke Cellars PAGE 11
1428 Keyneton Road,
Keyneton SA 5353
Ph: (08) 8564 8223
www.henschke.com.au

Hobbs of Barossa Ranges PAGE 96
550 Flaxman's Valley Road,
Angaston SA 5353
Ph: 0427 177 740
www.hobbsvintners.com.au

Hugh Hamilton Wines PAGE 97
94 McMurtrie Road,
McLaren Vale SA 5171
Ph: (08) 8323 8689
www.hughhamiltonwines.com.au

Jack Estate PAGE 34
15025 Riddoch Highway,
Coonawarra SA 5263
Ph: (08) 8736 3130
www.jackestate.com.au

Jeanneret Wines PAGE 108
Jeanneret Road, Sevenhill SA 5453
Ph: (08) 8843 4308
www.jeanneretwines.com

Jim Barry Wines PAGE 111
33 Craig Hill Road, Clare SA 5453
Ph: (08) 8842 2261
www.jimbarry.com

Kaesler Wines PAGES 114, 115
Barossa Valley Way,
Nuriootpa SA 5355
Ph: (08) 8562 4488
www.kaesler.com.au

Kangarilla Road Winery PAGE 106
44 Hamilton Road,
McLaren Flat SA 5171
Ph: (08) 8383 0533
www.kangarillaroad.com.au

Koonara Wines PAGE 58
44 Church Street, Penola SA 5277
Ph: (08) 8737 3222
www.koonara.com

Lake Breeze PAGES 31, 191
Step Road, Langhorne Creek SA 5255
Ph: (08) 8537 3017
www.lakebreeze.com.au

Lobethal Road Wines PAGE 164
2254 Onkaparinga Valley Road,
Mt Torrens SA 5244
Ph: (08) 8389 4595
www.lobethalroad.com

Mad Bastard Wines PAGE 67
Lot 2, Main North Road,
Clare SA 5453
Ph: 0418 809 389
www.madbastard.com.au

Majella Wines PAGE 66
Lynn Road, Coonawarra SA 5263
Ph: (08) 8736 3055
www.majellawines.com.au

Maxwell Wines PAGE 183
1 Olivers Road,
McLaren Vale SA 5171
Ph: (08) 8323 8200
www.maxwellwines.com.au

Mt Lofty Ranges Vineyard PAGE 188
166 Harris Road, Lenswood SA 5240
Ph: (08) 8389 8339
www.mtloftyrangesvineyard.com.au

Murray Street Vineyards PAGE 78
Murray Street, Greenock SA 5360
Ph: (08) 8562 8373
www.murraystreet.com.au

Paxton PAGES 5, 69
68 Wheaton Road,
McLaren Vale SA 5171
Ph: (08) 8323 9131
www.paxtonvineyards.com

Peter Seppelt Wines, Grand Cru Est PAGES 82, 83
Lot 274, Laubes Road,
Springton SA 5235
Ph: (08) 8568 2452
www.peterseppeltwines.com.au

Redman Wines PAGE 27
14830 Riddoch Highway,
Coonawarra SA 5263
Ph: (08) 8736 3331
www.redman.com.au

RockBare PAGE 186
102 Main Street, Hahndorf SA 5245
Ph: (08) 8388 7155
www.rockbare.com.au

SOUTH AUSTRALIA *continued*

Rymill Coonawarra PAGE 15
Riddoch Highway,
Coonawarra SA 5263
Ph: (08) 8736 5001
www.rymill.com.au

Saltram PAGE 187
Nuriootpa Road,
Angaston SA 5353
Ph: (08) 8561 0200
www.saltramwines.com.au

Samuel's Gorge PAGES 3, 38, 39
193 Chaffeys Road,
McLaren Vale SA 5171
Ph: (08) 8323 8651
www.gorge.com.au

Seppeltsfield Wines PAGE 8
Seppeltsfield Road,
Seppeltsfield SA 5355
Ph: (08) 8568 6200
www.seppeltsfield.com.au

Serafino Wines PAGE 68
39 Kangarilla Road,
McLaren Vale SA 5171
Ph: (08) 8323 0157
www.serafino.com.au

Shottesbrooke Vineyards
PAGE 74
101 Bagshaws Road,
McLaren Flat SA 5171
Ph: (08) 8383 0002
www.shottesbrooke.com.au

Skillogalee PAGE 71
Trevarrick Road, Sevenhill 5453
Ph: (08) 8843 4311
www.skillogalee.com.au

Sons of Eden PAGE 172
290 Penrice Road,
Angaston SA 5353
Ph: (08) 8564 2363
www.sonsofeden.com

Teusner Wines PAGES 89, 90, 91
Cnr Railway Terrace and
Research Road,
Nuriootpa SA 5352
Ph: (08) 8562 4147
www.teusner.com.au

The Lane PAGE 70
Ravenswood Lane,
Hahndorf SA 5245
Ph: (08) 8388 1250
www.thelane.com.au

Torbreck Vintners PAGE 75
348 Roennfeldt Road,
Marananga SA 5355
Ph: (08) 8562 4155
www.torbreck.com

Whistler Wines PAGES 44, 45
241 Seppeltsfield Road,
Marananga SA 5355
Ph: (08) 8562 4942
www.whistlerwines.com

Wirra Wirra Vineyards PAGE 56
McMurtrie Road,
McLaren Vale SA 5171
Ph: (08) 8323 8414
www.wirrawirra.com.au

Wolf Blass Wines PAGE 16
97 Sturt Highway,
Nuriootpa SA 5355
Ph: (08) 8568 7311
www.wolfblasswines.com

**Wynns Coonawarra
Estate** PAGE 77
Memorial Drive,
Coonawarra SA 5263
Ph: (08) 8736 2222
www.wynns.com.au

TASMANIA

Derwent Estate Wines PAGE 19
329 Lyell Highway,
Granton TAS 7030
Ph: (03) 6263 5802
www.derwentestate.com.au

Ghost Rock Vineyard PAGE 76
1055 Port Sorell Road,
Northdown TAS 7307
Ph: (03) 6428 4005
www.ghostrock.com.au

Holm Oak Vineyard PAGE 99
11 West Bay Road,
Rowella TAS 7270
Ph: (03) 6394 7577
www.holmoakvineyards.com.au

Home Hill Winery PAGES 142, 143
38 Nairn Street,
Ranelagh TAS 7109
Ph: (03) 6264 1200
www.homehillwines.com.au

Moores Hill Estate PAGE 88
3343 West Tamar Highway,
Sidmouth TAS 7270
Ph: (03) 6394 7649
www.mooreshill.com.au

Moorilla PAGES 6, 57
655 Main Road,
Berriedale TAS 7011
Ph: (03) 6277 9960
www.moorilla.com.au

Pipers Brook Vineyard PAGE 119
1216 Pipers Brook Road,
Pipers Brook TAS 7254
Ph: (03) 6382 7527
www.pipersbrook.com

Puddleduck Vineyard PAGE 94
992 Richmond Road,
Richmond TAS 7025
Ph: (03) 6260 2301
www.puddleduck.com.au

Stefano Lubiana Wines PAGE 93
60 Rowbottoms Road,
Granton TAS 7030
Ph: (03) 6263 7457
www.slw.com.au

VICTORIA

All Saints Estate PAGE 52
All Saints Road,
Wahgunyah VIC 3687
Ph: (02) 6035 2222
www.allsaintswine.com.au

Best's Great Western PAGE 109
111 Best's Road,
Great Western VIC 3374
Ph: (03) 5356 2250
www.bestswines.com

Blue Pyrenees Estate PAGE 168
Vinoca Road, Avoca VIC 3467
Ph: (03) 5465 1111
www.bluepyrenees.com.au

Boat O'Craigo PAGE 112
458 Maroondah Highway,
Healesville VIC 3777
Ph: (03) 5962 6899
www.boatocraigo.com.au

Brown Brothers PAGE 129
239 Milawa-Bobinawarrah Road,
Milawa VIC 3678
Ph: (03) 5720 5500
www.brownbrothers.com.au

Campbells Winery PAGE 18
4603 Murray Valley Highway,
Rutherglen VIC 3685
Ph: (02) 6033 6000
www.campbellswines.com.au

**Captains Creek
Organic Wines** PAGE 118
Kangaroo Hills Road,
Blampied VIC 3364
Ph: (03) 5345 7408
www.captainscreek.com

Crittenden Estate PAGE 110
25 Harrisons Road,
Dromana VIC 3936
Ph: (03) 5981 8322
www.crittendenwines.com.au

Curly Flat Vineyard PAGES 104, 105
263 Collivers Road,
Lancefield VIC 3435
Ph: (03) 5429 1956
www.curlyflat.com

**De Bortoli Wines
(Yarra Valley)** PAGE 33
58 Pinnacle Lane,
Dixons Creek VIC 3775
Ph: (03) 5965 2271
www.debortoli.com.au

Domaine Chandon PAGE 173
727 Maroondah Highway,
Coldstream VIC 3770
Ph: (03) 9738 9200
www.domainechandon.com.au

Dominique Portet PAGE 113
870 Maroondah Highway,
Coldstream VIC 3770
Ph: (03) 5962 5760
www.dominiqueportet.com

Ellender Estate PAGE 54
260 Green Gully Road,
Glenlyon VIC 3461
Ph: (03) 5348 7785
www.ellenderwines.com.au

Fergusson Winery PAGE 17
82 Wills Road, Yarra Glen VIC 3775
Ph: (03) 5965 2237
www.fergussonwinery.com.au

**Giant Steps / Innocent
Bystander** PAGE 26
336 Maroondah Highway,
Healesville VIC 3777
Ph: (03) 5962 6111
www.innocentbystander.com.au

Hanging Rock Winery PAGES 48, 49
88 Jim Road, Newham VIC 3442
Ph: (03) 5427 0542
www.hangingrock.com.au

Harcourt Valley Vineyards PAGE 12
3339 Harmony Way,
Harcourt VIC 3453
Ph: (03) 5474 2223
www.harcourtvalley.com.au

Heathcote Winery PAGE 128
185 High Street,
Heathcote VIC 3523
Ph: (03) 5433 2595
www.heathcotewinery.com.au

**Immerse in the
Yarra Valley** PAGE 180
1548 Melba Highway,
Dixons Creek VIC 3775
Ph: (03) 5965 2444
www.immerse.com.au

Indigo Vineyard PAGE 155
1221 Beechworth-Wangaratta Road,
Everton Upper VIC 3678
Ph: (03) 5727 0233
www.indigovineyard.com.au

Levantine Hill Estate PAGES 84, 85
882 Maroondah Highway,
(Corner of Hill Road)
Coldstream VIC 3770
Ph: (03) 5962 1333
www.levantinehill.com.au

Mitchelton Wines PAGE 121
470 Mitchellstown Road,
Nagambie VIC 3608
Ph: (03) 5736 2222
www.mitchelton.com.au

Oakridge Wines PAGE 169
864 Maroondah Highway,
Coldstream VIC 3770
Ph: (03) 9738 9900
www.oakridgewines.com.au

**Scion Vineyard
and Winery** PAGE 37
74 Slaughterhouse Road,
Rutherglen VIC 3685
Ph: (02) 6032 8844
www.scionvineyard.com

Seppelt Great Western PAGE 122
36 Cemetery Road,
Great Western VIC 3374
Ph: (03) 5361 2239
www.seppelt.com.au

Seville Estate PAGE 117
65 Linwood Road,
Seville VIC 3139
Ph: (03) 5964 2622
www.sevilleestate.com.au

Shadowfax Wines PAGE 36
K Road, Werribee VIC 3030
Ph: (03) 9731 4420
www.shadowfax.com.au

Simão & Co. Wines PAGE 42
PO Box 231, Rutherglen VIC 3685
Ph: 0439 459 183
www.simaoandco.com.au

**Stanton and Killeen
Wines** PAGE 43
440 Jacks Road,
Rutherglen VIC 3685
Ph: (02) 6032 9457
www.stantonandkilleenwines.com.au

Warrabilla Wines PAGE 10
6152 Murray Valley Highway,
Rutherglen VIC 3685
Ph: (02) 6035 7242
www.warrabillawines.com.au

Warramunda Estate PAGE 126
860 Maroondah Highway,
Coldstream VIC 3770
Ph: 0412 694 394
www.warramundaestate.com.au

Wine by Farr PAGE 120
293 Russell Road,
Bannockburn VIC 3331
Ph: (03) 5281 1733
www.byfarr.com.au

Zonzo Estate Yarra Valley PAGE 139
957 Healesville-Yarra Glen Road,
Yarra Glen VIC 3775
Ph: (03) 9730 2500
www.zonzo.com.au

WESTERN AUSTRALIA

Barreca's Wines PAGE 146
Lot 19001, South Western Highway,
Donnybrook WA 6239
Ph: (08) 9731 1716

Bettenay Wines PAGE 23
248 Tom Cullity Drive,
Cowaramup WA 6284
Ph: (08) 9755 5539
www.bettenaywines.com.au

Brookland Valley Estate PAGE 116
4070 Caves Road,
Wilyabrup WA 6284
Ph: (08) 9755 6042
www.brooklandvalley.com.au

Cape Mentelle PAGE 86
331 Wallcliffe Road,
Margaret River WA 6285
Ph: (08) 9757 0888
www.capementelle.com.au

**Cape Naturaliste
Vineyard** PAGE 156
1 Coley Road, Yallingup WA 6282
Ph: (08) 9755 2538
www.capenaturalistevineyard.com.au

**Coward & Black
at Providore** PAGE 32
448 Harmans South Road,
Wilyabrup WA 6280
Ph: (08) 9755 6355
www.cowardandblack.com.au

Estate 807 PAGES 136, 137
807 Scotsdale Road,
Denmark WA 6333
Ph: (08) 9840 9027
www.estate807.com.au

Flying Fish Cove PAGE 41
Lot 125, Caves Road,
Wilyabrup WA 6280
Ph: (08) 9755 6600
www.flyingfishcove.com.au

Fraser Gallop Estate PAGE 123
547 Metricup Road,
Wilyabrup WA 6285
Ph: (08) 9755 7553
www.fgewines.com.au

Happs and Three Hills PAGE 53
575 Commonage Road,
Quindalup WA 6281
Ph: (08) 9755 3300
www.happs.com.au

Hay Shed Hill Wines PAGE 138
511 Harmans Mill Road,
Wilyabrup WA 6280
Ph: (08) 9755 6046
www.hayshedhill.com.au

House of Cards PAGE 150
Cnr Caves and Quininup Road,
Yallingup WA 6282
Ph: (08) 9755 2583
www.houseofcardswine.com.au

Howard Park Wines PAGE 160
543 Miamup Road,
Cowaramup WA 6284
Ph: (08) 9756 5200
www.burchfamilywines.com.au

Ironwood Estate Wines PAGE 161
2191 Porongurup Road,
Porongurup WA 6324
Ph: (08) 9853 1126
www.ironwoodestatewines.com.au

Juniper Estate PAGE 158
98 Tom Cullity Drive,
Cowaramup WA 6284
Ph: (08) 9755 9000
www.juniperestate.com.au

Leeuwin Estate PAGES 170, 171
Stevens Road,
Margaret River WA 6285
Ph: (08) 9759 0000
www.leeuwinestate.com.au

Lenton Brae PAGE 174
3887 Caves Road,
Wilyabrup, WA 6285
Ph: (08) 9755 6255
www.lentonbrae.com

Sandalford Wines PAGE 152
777 Metricup Road,
Wilyabrup WA 6280
Ph: (08) 9755 6213
www.sandalford.com

Singlefile Wines PAGE 20
90 Walter Road,
Denmark WA 6333
Ph: (08) 9840 9749
www.singlefilewines.com

**The Lake House
Denmark** PAGE 154
106 Turner Road,
Denmark WA 6333
Ph: (08) 9848 2444
www.lakehousedenmark.com.au

Vasse Felix PAGE 87
Cnr Tom Cullity Drive
and Caves Road
Cowaramup WA 6284
Ph: (08) 9756 5000
www.vassefelix.com.au

Voyager Estate PAGES 80, 81
1 Stevens Road,
Margaret River WA 6285
Ph: (08) 9757 6354
www.voyagerestate.com.au

West Cape Howe Wines
PAGES 46, 47
14923 Muir Highway,
Mount Barker WA 6234
Ph: (08) 9892 1444
www.westcapehowewines.com.au

Whicher Ridge Wines PAGE 184
200 Chapman Hill East Road,
Chapman Hill WA 6280
Ph: (08) 9753 1394
www.whicherridge.com.au

Wills Domain PAGE 176
Brash Road, Yallingup WA 6282
Ph: (08) 9755 2327
www.willsdomain.com.au

Windows Estate PAGE 59
4 Quininup Road,
Yallingup WA 6282
Ph: (08) 9756 6655
www.windowsestate.com

Woody Nook Wines PAGE 140
506 Metricup Road,
Wilyabrup WA 6280
Ph: (08) 9755 7547
www.woodynook.com.au

WINE DOGS BREED INDEX

WINE DOGS AUSTRALIA 4
ISBN 978-1-921336-48-5

DESIGNED BY SUSAN ELLIOTT, COPYRIGHT © McGILL DESIGN GROUP PTY LTD, 2015

ALL PHOTOGRAPHY © CRAIG McGILL, 2015
WITH THE EXCEPTION OF PAGE 101 (ISTOCK.COM) AND PAGE 192 © SUSAN ELLIOTT

BARREL ARTWORK ON PAGES 5 AND 69 © MEGAN O'HARA

EDITING AND PROOFREADING BY VICKY FISHER

PRINTED BY 1010 PRINTING INTERNATIONAL LIMITED, CHINA.

PUBLISHED BY GIANT DOG, ABN 27 110 894 178.
PO BOX 964, ROZELLE NSW 2039 AUSTRALIA
TELEPHONE: (+612) 9555 4077
WWW.WINEDOGS.COM

FOR ORDERS: ORDERS@WINEDOGS.COM

OPINIONS EXPRESSED IN WINE DOGS AUSTRALIA 4 ARE NOT NECESSARILY THOSE OF THE PUBLISHER.

OTHER TITLES BY CRAIG McGILL AND SUSAN ELLIOTT INCLUDE:
WINE DOGS: ORIGINAL EDITION – THE DOGS OF AUSTRALIAN WINERIES ISBN 0-9580856-1-7
WINE DOGS: DELUXE EDITION – THE DOGS OF AUSTRALASIAN WINERIES ISBN 0-9580856-2-5
FOOTY DOGS: THE DOGS OF AUSTRALIAN RULES FOOTBALL ISBN 0-9580856-3-3
WINE DOGS AUSTRALIA – MORE DOGS FROM AUSTRALIAN WINERIES ISBN 978-1-921336-02-7
WINE DOGS AUSTRALIA 2 – MORE DOGS FROM AUSTRALIAN WINERIES ISBN 978-1-921336-16-4
WINE DOGS AUSTRALIA 3 – MORE DOGS FROM AUSTRALIAN WINERIES ISBN 978-1-921336-28-7
WINE DOGS: USA EDITION – THE DOGS OF NORTH AMERICAN WINERIES ISBN 0-9580856-6-8
WINE DOGS USA 2 – MORE DOGS FROM NORTH AMERICAN WINERIES ISBN 978-1-921336-10-2
WINE DOGS USA 3 – MORE DOGS FROM NORTH AMERICAN WINERIES ISBN 978-1-921336-29-4
WINE DOGS CALIFORNIA ISBN 978-1-921336-43-0
WINE DOGS ITALY – THE DOGS OF ITALIAN WINERIES ISBN 978-1-921336-11-9
WINE DOGS NEW ZEALAND – THE DOGS OF NEW ZEALAND WINERIES ISBN 978-1-921336-12-6
WINE DOGS NEW ZEALAND 2 ISBN 978-1-921336-49-2
WINE CATS ISBN 978-1-921336-38-6

HEALTH WARNING: VETERINARY ASSOCIATIONS ADVISE THAT EATING GRAPES, SULTANAS OR RAISINS CAN
MAKE A DOG EXTREMELY ILL AND COULD POSSIBLY RESULT IN FATAL KIDNEY FAILURE. IN THE INTERESTS OF
CANINE HEALTH AND WELLBEING, DO NOT FEED YOUR DOG GRAPES OR ANY GRAPE BY-PRODUCT.